OTHER BOOKS BY MARILYN HACKER

SELECTED POEMS

1965–1990

SELECTED POEMS

1965–1990

MARILYN HACKER

W · W · NORTON & COMPANY

NEW YORK · LONDON

FIRST EDITION

The text of this book is composed in Palatino with the display set in Palatino and Weiss Initials. Composition and manufacturing by the Maple-Vail Book Manufacturing Group. Book design by Marjorie J. Flock.

Grateful acknowledgment is made to the editors and publishers of the following books, in which the poems in this collection first appeared:

The Viking Press, for poems from *Presentation Piece*, 1974;

Alfred A. Knopf, for poems from *Separations*, 1976, *Taking Notice*, 1980, and *Assumptions*, 1985;

Random House, for poems from *Going Back to the River*, 1990.

Poems from *Taking Notice* and *Assumptions* were also included in *The Hang-Glider's Daughter*, published by Onlywomen Press (UK) in 1990.

Library of Congress Cataloging-in-Publication Data
Hacker, Marilyn, 1942–
    [Poems. Selections]
    Selected poems / Marilyn Hacker.
        p.   cm.
    1. Mothers and daughters—Poetry. 2. Lesbians—Poetry.
3. Women—Poetry.   I. Title.
PS3558.A28A6   1994
811'.54—dc20   94-27507

ISBN 0-393-03675-8

W. W. Norton & Company, Inc., 500 Fifth Avenue, New York, N.Y. 10110
W. W. Norton & Company Ltd., 10 Coptic Street, London WC1A 1PU

1 2 3 4 5 6 7 8 9 0

for Richard Howard, for Robyn Selman,
and, in all seasons, for Karyn J. London

CONTENTS

F R O M

TAKING NOTICE

1 9 8 0

F R O M

PRESENTATION PIECE

1 9 7 4

Presentation Piece

About the skull of the beloved, filled
with unlikely innocence, liver pâté,
tidbits in aspic. You were never
anybody's "lover," should live
in staterooms full of temporary homage.
The corridor slants, cradled on the
crest of an
earthquake. Far above, smokestacks
proceed through badlands of snapped bridges.

About the skull of the beloved, filled
with a perilous remedy, sloshing
into the corners of the damp eyes
where you are reflected, twice, upside
down. The last image before
death is recorded photographically
on the retina for half an hour.
Prints can be made. The darkroom
is at the end of the corridor.

"These are worlds that were his thighs." You are
the assistant purser, translating
and filing telegraphic messages. "Arriving
Thursday 2 P.M." "Take another little
piece of my heart now baby." "Armed and awaiting
signal before tides change." One of the messages
may be for you. "In an affluent society
cannibalism
is a sexual predilection."

That is not fresh meat. It was kept overnight
in a tub of brine. Hand remembers
the ribs' wet parting, the heavy pulse on the palm.
This is not the door to the engine room
though a pulse whines in the walls.
Green velvet ropes enlace a green
velvet chaise-longue, beneath
the purple jewels of the parvenue
empress. Meet me tonight under your tongue.

There is no easy way up. Bite
on your lip; do you taste what I do?
A gold skewer
pierces and joins his hands; the handle
is a five-leafed rose. Let me live
in your mouth; I know a place
where the earlobe is imperfectly joined to the skull.
At sunrise
we can look across the wasted sea for miles.

Exiles

Her brown falcon perches above the sink
as steaming water forks over my hands.
Below the wrists they shrivel and turn pink.
I am in exile in my own land.

Her half-grown cats scuffle across the floor
trailing a slime of blood from where they fed.
I lock the door. They claw under the door.
I am in exile in my own bed.

Her spotted mongrel, bristling with red mange,
sleeps on the threshold of the Third Street bar
where I drink brandy as the couples change.
I am in exile where my neighbors are.

On the pavement, cans of ashes burn.
Her green lizard scuttles from the light
around torn cardboard charred to glowing fern.
I am in exile in my own sight.

Her blond child sits on the stoop when I
come back at night. Cold hands, blue lids; we both
need sleep. She tells me she is going to die.
I am in exile in my own youth.

Lady of distances, this fire, this water,
this earth make sanctuary where I stand.
Call off your animals and your blond daughter.
I am in exile in my own hands.

She Bitches About Boys

To live on charm, one must be courteous.
To live on others' love, one must be lovable.
Some get away with murder being beautiful.

Girls love a sick child or a healthy animal.
A man who's both itches them like an incubus,
but I, for one, have had a bellyful

of giving reassurances and obvious
advice with scrambled eggs and cereal;
then bad debts, broken dates, and lecherous

onanistic dreams of estival
nights when some high-strung, well-hung, penurious
boy, not knowing what he'd get, could be more generous.

from The Navigators

I

Between us on our wide bed we cuddle an incubus
whom we have filled with voyages. We wake
more apart than before, with open hands.
Your stomach and my head begin to ache.
We cannot work. You are in pain. I cry.
Outside the dirty window, in the damp
film of new spring, muddy brown children dabble
cardboard in puddles, chalk across a wall
where two boys on a fire escape eat oranges.
Love, longing makes us both anonymous,
middle-aged, quarrelsome, ridiculous.
You hurt for want of tears. I cry for pain.

Real, grimy and exiled, he
eludes us.
I would show him books and bridges,
and make a language we could all speak.

No blond fantasy
Mother has sent to plague us in the spring,
he has his own bad dreams, needs work, gets drunk,
maybe would not have chosen to be beautiful.

Because we held him while he screamed or threw up,
were good in bed, or good for a hot meal,
we were not given his life by the scruff of its neck
or even the right to speak too much out of turn.
Love, my love, is not what you have done
but what you are just now doing.

Oh, I would hold his head and feed him oranges
to taste his warm home,
pink shrimp to taste the green lick of the sea.
To taste the road, tart cold wild apples
and long pale grapes with dusty moon skins.
To taste my love, amber Greek honey
that coats his tongue with sweet thinking of bitter.
To taste my love, raw meat, radishes, lemons
and salt rubbing his lips where they are broken.

III

You made an algebra: his tastes in food,
when the dinner guests would be too much
for him to keep his poise, his surly moods;
to calculate how often you could touch
the real boy like your dream sharing our bed,
one arm sprawled off the mattress near your head.
He slept. Your hands relaxed around his chest,
and all the ambiguities could rest
between your shoulder and his shoulder blades.
I saw you move your mouth against his nape,
wanting to wake him in your arms, afraid
of how his face would age coming awake.

IV

His Wife at Bellevue

Trackless and lost between piss-colored walls,
she huddles on the bench arm, hides her face,
shakes with sobs or dry retching. The intern calls
names in a bored voice. People shift in place.
Clocks sweep toward morning and she hides her face.
Between the red-felt collar and her hair,
her neck is cracked with white beneath the brown.

I draw an old man. Three boys turn to stare
over their bench to see what I have down;
one has a bloody gash beneath his hair.
I am a stranger whom she cannot trust.
She hid her face and let me bring her here.
My hand quiets her trembling. Since she must
feel some hand on her sickness and her fear,
my hand is on her shoulder; we are here.

V

Across the mud flats and the wide roads, over rivers and
  borders,
by bus, truck, trailer, car and foot,
my two loves have gone, the dark and the fair.
Truck drivers, salesmen, schoolgirls on vacation
taste the salt fruit of their bodies.
They breathe strange air; strange hands press their
  shoulders,
strange voices speak to them.
Mother of exiles, save them from wind and rage.
Mother of journeys, let the sea be kind to them.

Along the highway, despair and dead animals
steam on the macadam. Sheet-white, the sky
closes them in. Miles apart, in a mud-wide state,
they sing out loud, and the long road is empty
from red hill to scrub bush. Branches are bare with heat
and it's only May. Home and the ports
swing like a compass needle, both far away.
Mother of exiles, save them from wind and rage.
Mother of journeys, let the sea be kind to them.

Together, briefly, they sit on splintered pilings.
Thick, spit-yellow foam slaps the diesel hulls.

Storms are in the gulf; the catch is north.
North on an old coast, landlocked on my island
dry in soot-thick summer, I spin their warmth.
I loop their names in words. One road is closed
to women and conspirators. I plot. I sing.
Mother of exiles, save them from wind and rage.
Mother of journeys, let the sea be kind to them.

VI

When you told me that he was in jail
again, I scrounged two hundred for his bail
in two hours, wired it down, came home, threw up,
cried while you brewed me coffee, and threw up,
and threw up every thirty minutes flat
for two days, till the airline ended that
and flew him back. Pale, tired, clean,
I took the Carey bus at two-fifteen
and waited at the terminal for him.
He had new, checked, pegged slacks. They'd cropped his
        hair.
He said he was surprised that I was there
and had I dieted to get so thin.
He asked why you weren't there, and I said, well,
you were engaging in diplomacy
and would be waiting up at the hotel;
which meant, you had to wait around and see
his wife. We took the bus back. It was dark
inside, but floodlit girders looped the park.
Grained, heavy cones of light spilled on the sky
as planes dropped to their runways through the mist.
There was a groan of engines as we kissed
and searchlights limned my hand over his thigh.

Seventy-Second Street; so tired it hurt.
The florid Slav bursting his dirty shirt

could see from the cash window what we were,
a trio of unluggaged travelers
wanting cheap beds and anonymity.
You signed for two, although he could see three.
Two bulldykes teased an acrid teenage whore
pinioned with dexies to the lobby door
and wondered if distinction could be made
among us, who was trick and who was trade.

The walls were hotel green. Someone had drawn
blue crayon mountains facing the iron bed.
We shelved our change of underwear. I yawned.
A swish of cars, a whiff of the dried dead
came through the blinded courtyard to the halls.
You went away that night. The tangled sheets
were heaped and ribboned underneath our feet.
I held him combed in foreign sounds. Thin walls
enclose nocturnal lexicons. He dreamed
of walls, baked concrete glaring at the sun.
Thick sewage sucked his chest. A milky gleam
slid on the trustee's buttons, and the gun
barrel cocked on his hip swelled twice its size.
(I ground my fists in pillows, reading him.)
He threw his hands up to protect his eyes
and woke knocking his elbow on my chin.

X

Orpheus and animus,
drawing back to journeys now,
leaving me on shores behind
streets and shutters of the mind
as a new October streaks
dry hollows underneath our cheeks:
All that I have learned from you,
all that I have failed to learn,

I will order up again
with an overcautious pen,
making models, giving names
(nothing ever stays the same),
initiate the change that moves
the peripheries of love.

For Elektra

My father dies again in dreams, a twin.
She stands above his dying like a small
vulture in curlers, twisting her veined hands,
knowing he died before. Loose-limbed in under-
     wear,
he slips from indolence to agony
on a rumpled double bed. His round
face flattens with pain. I, overgrown,
watch and fall distant till the dark green wall
is tentative beneath my palm. I fill the window light.
He is my father and my father's twin,
dying again. She did not kill or save him
with her dry hands. She does not touch him now.
The screech of her nails on my cheek. I presume
too much in giving you my mother monster
rehashed in pincurls from a guilty dream
where she slaps my hand for taking cakes and cocks
on my plate and failing, failing.
I will speak to you. You are not my brother,
unmasked on the river path as I long for exile.
Those black figures on the snow, too simply
dark fingers on a white thigh, establish
the clean hierarchic myth.
                        Brothers and brothers
pass under, pass over, but I never had
a brother. Lustful shorthaired virgin
bitch borrows the voice and says,
"Your Mother is my mother. Dare."
How she bores me with her metaphors.
I would rather make love and poems than kill
my mother. "So would I. Have you done

flaunting your cunt and your pen in her face
when she's not looking? High above your bed,
like a lamppost with eyes, stern as a pay toilet,
she stands, waiting to be told off
and tolled out." Waiting to be told off,
Miss Bitch puts me to work for nothing
at being my own brother, with such sisters.

Elektra on Third Avenue

for Link

At six, when April chills our hands and feet
walking downtown, we stop at Clancy's Bar
or Bickford's, where the part-time hustlers are,
scoffing between the mailroom and the street.
Old pensioners appraise them while they eat,
and so do we, debating half in jest
which piece of hasty pudding we'd like best.
I know you know I think your mouth is sweet
as anything exhibited for sale,
fresh coffee cake or boys fresh out of jail,
which tender hint of incest brings me near
to ordering more coffee or more beer.
The homebound crowd provides more youth to cruise.
We nurse our cups, nudge knees, and pick and choose.

The Art of the Novel

for Bill Brodecky

The afternoon breaks from a pale
morning on the water of maps
hanging above the desk. Cities
interest him more than people. Geography
is a kind of vast gossip. I always
gossip in poems, mostly about myself,
hinting at inadmissible longings.
I want Everything. Every day
this week I woke up so happy
I felt guilty; warm legs
wrapped around mine. I can't
stay in this beautiful city forever.

I am inventing a city
in these lines. The people
are half real, living
in my correspondent city, created
for them with streets and buildings,
trees and the necessary harbor.
They frequent a bar and perhaps a beach, but I
take them from one place to the other.
You can draw an accurate map and say:
This is where *she* lives with her young German
from Buenos Aires. Five blocks away
in a converted carriage house with a back garden
lives an older painter who covets them both,
usually confusing love and politics.

It is almost always a spring morning. Will I ever
start to work early? We remember the pale
profile out of Goethe. He can't
make his head a compass, disparages maps
and gets seasick on Green Street. I have land legs
now, imagining a network of double cities
from here to Leningrad. I might be happy
writing novels, if I could color into geography
like the plate of fruit I painted yesterday.
It is almost always
a spring morning, in the air a longing
to confuse myself.

Before the War

We are asleep under mirrors. What do I
look like? Your mouth
opens on a dream of altered landscapes.
Hidden in the Iron Mountains,
the adolescent general is in love
with you. Noon light stands in the window,
cloudy and white. They are using mustard gas.
That night child anarchists besieged the corners.
Tin cans exploded in front of us; rhythm
escaped in the blistered rain. Everyone
was hungry. You sound
like that in the morning, someone
told her on the telephone, and all
the bar heard it Friday night.
Culled from a garden in Pacific Heights,
the charred corpse of her last lover, ankles crossed
at a vulnerable and tender angle,
embellishes the service porch
above an architecture of dead boys.
It happens every morning at the gas
station while we are still asleep
around the pillow like a third lover.
Covered in burning Saran Wrap,
the young attendant knocks the telephone
off the hook, crashes through
the plate-glass window
and flames out like a screaming Bunsen burner
under the open hood of a '39
Renault sedan. I wake up with your elbow
under my neck. Come here.
Tell me what that eruption on the sun
is.

The Sea Coming Indoors

The war is far away, sweet
birdsong around the villas on the cliff.
Breakers crash below the dining room
where a gawky Filipina girl
rearranges and rearranges
silver forks on a white linen cloth.
I have given her
your skin, but your mouth
curves around a secret. Speak.
Tapping the salad forks
on her thin left wrist, she paces
the length of the window; a yard away
the drop behind glass
turns her stomach, and a vision
recurs: she is climbing down
the cliff in a gold dress, loose rocks
and thorn bushes bite her palms, these new
shoes will slip, little slides
of dirt and pebbles brush her ankles.
                                              You
will not come back, decked
with garnets and thorn bushes, hefting
a live grenade. When
you take off your shirt, I see
a line of tiny rubies set
in the central furrow of your chest.
See, my hands are empty. I close
my eyes and forget what I am holding.
You are not here. Gem grains
crease my palm. I am looking at you.
Salt air wreaths the door as it opens.

A gap flickers in skin. Elegant
insects twitch to life
in rock shells on the slope. She huddles
on a ledge, unfolding
like a kite before herself unfolding
her hands. It is too late. The seeds
of her disease cling to her wet palms
at the edges of vision. I am sitting
in front of the window, counting
silverware. I have given her
your skin.

Pornographic Poem

You are walking
down the corridor. A man
in striped boxer shorts comes
out closing the last door. It is
the bathroom. Not really
the last door; the corridor
turns there. Your room
is beyond the turn. The third
door on the left. A blond
boy with long hair in faded
jeans and no shirt walks out of the
bathroom, turns. The man
passes you as the boy turns; he
has a crew cut. You are sweating,
your feet are damp in old sandals.
There are no windows in the corridor;
it is underground. Below it
is another corridor, and below
that. Above it
is another corridor. You think
of the window in your room. You can
have a window because of the
hill. At night, if you are
alone, you explore
levels you have not yet seen, under
the DC bulbs. Sometimes
you pass a person on the dark stairs, but
usually not. Barefoot
on the faded figured rug, you can
stop in front of a closed door, hear
a saucepan clank on a hot plate, skin

sliding in sheets, somebody
swallowing, coughing. You always
save the last level for next time. Old men
stay on the upper
levels. A tanned
young man with curly black hair
goes into the bathroom. You
slow down. You go into
the bathroom.

Forage Sestina

This is for your body hidden in words
moving through a crumbling structure.
Between heaps of plaster, chicken wire
snaggles the gaping floor. Stripped of beams,
cement encloses more cement. A wall
mounds up between parlor and dining room.

Explicit shadows grapple through the room
which is a ruined city. Falling words
erode veined gullies in the nearer wall.
This is to see if only structure
communicates. Under a beam
an outlet spouts tongues of stripped wire.

and your breath crackles like a shorted wire.
You are standing behind me, even in this room
which is a camouflage. Signal beams
flash through the casement, and our words
cadence them, shushed with light, making a structure
of light and sound bouncing off the bare wall.

I want to touch you, but you are the wall
crumbling, the report over the wire
service that there were no survivors. Structure
demands that we remain inside the room,
that you cannot be hedged in easy words
like skin or hands, that we cannot look through the beams

of the burnt roof and see stars. All the beams
were hauled off. Concrete floor, ceiling, walls
surround us. There is one window. Words

cannot be trusted. Capillaries wire
swiveling eyes. If we search this room
we may be able to plot out the structure

of the whole building. We were told that the structure
is flawed, that the searchlight beam
from the bridge pierces cracks. If the room
begins to rotate, floor becoming wall
et cetera, and white sparks dribble from torn wires,
there has been a rebellion of words.

Words will peel off you, revealing the structure
of a human body branched with wires. Over the last beam
keeping the sky from the walls, vines drip into the room.

Sestina

for D. G. B.

For a week now our bodies have whispered
together, telling each other secrets
you and I would keep. Their language,
harder and more tender than this, wakes
us suddenly in the half dawn, tangled
dragons on their map. They have a plan.

We are stranded travelers who plan
to ditch our bags and walk. The hill wind whispers
danger and rain. We are going different ways. That tangled
thornbush is where the road forks. The secrets
we told on the station bench to keep awake
were lies. I suspect from your choice of language

that you are not speaking your native language.
You will not know about the city plan
tattooed behind my knee. But the skin wakes
up in humming networks, audibly whispers
over the dead wind. Everybody's secrets
jam the wires. Syllables get tangled

with bus tickets and matchbooks. You tangled
my hair in your fingers and language
split like a black fig. I suck the secrets
off your skin. This isn't in the plan,
the subcutaneous transmitter whispers.
Be circumspect. What sort of person wakes

up twice in a wrecked car? And we wake
in wary seconds of each other, tangled

damply together. Your cock whispers
inside my thigh that there is language
without memory. Your fingers plan
wet symphonies in my garrulous secret

places. There is nothing secret
in people crying at weddings and singing at wakes;
and when you pack a duffel bag and plan
on the gratuitous, you will still tangle
purpose and habit, more baggage, more language.
It is not accidental what they whisper.

Our bodies whispered under the sheet. Their secret
language will not elude us when we wake
into the tangled light without a plan.

Villanelle

Every day our bodies separate,
exploded torn and dazed.
Not understanding what we celebrate

we grope through languages and hesitate
and touch each other, speechless and amazed;
and every day our bodies separate

us further from our planned, deliberate
ironic lives. I am afraid, disphased,
not understanding what we celebrate

when our fused limbs and lips communicate
the unlettered power we have raised.
Every day our bodies' separate

routines are harder to perpetuate.
In wordless darkness we learn wordless praise,
not understanding what we celebrate;

wake to ourselves, exhausted, in the late
morning as the wind tears off the haze,
not understanding how we celebrate
our bodies. Every day we separate.

Sisterhood

for Dora FitzGerald

No place for a lady, this
backcountry gateway comes
up from dreams; the wounds
are an entrance, or a season ticket.
The morning freshness, the
summer's end mountain calm:
distractions. "What do you
call this town?"

No man will love you, no
woman be your friend, your
face will go away, your body
betray you. We wrestled
to the floor, his fingers
blanching my elbows, cords
popping his neck. Don't look
into the sun. Don't squint.

He lay on the concrete
ramp of the bus terminal. I
massaged his back and shoulders through his clothes.
I opened his trench coat, peeled
its collar away from his thin
white shirt, his thin chest.
Staining the slashed white
yellowish pink, those wounds.

When you give the ghost
bread and water he asks

for, you incur prophecy.
"Why have you come here,
woman? Your city
is far away. We do not speak
your language. Your sister
is dead.

"Take off your rings
at the first gate. At the second,
your crown of lapis lazuli.
You must leave your golden
breastplate at the third, and below
the gallows where he hangs
who forgot you, and will not rise,
break your mother's scepter."

They have killed him
often. He bled
on the concrete floor. My hands
were not healing. They took him
into the next room. I heard
gunshots. I woke screaming.
At the bottom of hell
he swings in the stinking wind. She watches.

We, women, never
trust his returnings. He takes
the bread and water, but
the words on the paper
are illegible. His body
lies severed on the white sand
and the pieces are not
food, they are stones.

We gather those
jewels and wear them,
lapis in the crown, amethysts
over the nipples, garnets
oozing on cool
fingers. The gateway
dreams itself up, and we eye the surly
guard, and strip, and go down.

Elegy

for Janis Joplin

Crying from exile, I
mourn you, dead singer, crooning and palming
your cold cheeks, calling you: You.
A man told me you died; he was
foreign, I felt for the first time, drunk, in his car, my
throat choked: You won't sing for me
now. Later I laughed in the hair between
his shoulder blades, well enough
loved in a narrow
bed; it was
your Southern Comfort
grin stretching my
mouth. You were in me
all night,

shouting our pain, sucking off
the mike, telling a strong-headed
woman's daily beads to dumb kids
creaming on your high
notes. Some morning at wolf hour
they'll know.
Stay in my
gut, woman lover I never
touched, tongued, or sang to; stay
in back of my
throat, sandpaper
velvet, Janis, you
overpaid your
dues, damn it, why are you dead?

Cough up your whiskey gut
demon, send him home howling
to Texas, to every
fat bristle-chinned
white motel keeper on
Route 66, every half-
Seminole waitress with a
crane's neck, lantern-jawed
truck driver missing a
finger joint, dirt farmer's
blond boy with asthma and sea dreams,
twenty-one-year-old
mother of three who got far
as Albuquerque once.

Your veins were
highways from
Coca-Cola flatland,
dust and dead
flies crusting the
car window till it rained.
Drive! anywhere
out of here, the
ratty upholstery smelling
of dog piss and cunt,
bald tires swiveled and
lurched on slicked macadam
skidding the funk in your mouth
to a Black woman's tongue.

Faggots and groupies and
meth heads loved you, you
loved bodies and booze
and hard work, and more
than that, fame. On your

left tit was a tattooed
valentine, around your
wrist a tattooed filigree; around
your honeycomb brain webbed
klieg lights and amp circuits screamed
Love Love and the booze-
scag-and-cocaine baby twisted your
box, kicked your
throat and the songs came.

I wanted to write your
blues, Janis, and put my
tongue in your mouth that way.
Lazy and grasping and
treacherous, beautiful
insomniac freaking the ceiling,
the cold smog went slowly blue, the cars
caught up with your heartbeat, maybe you were not
alone, but the ceiling told you
otherwise, and scag said:
You are more famous than anyone
out of East Texas, your hair is a
monument, your voice preserved
in honey, I love you, lie down.

I am in London and
you, more meat than Hollywood
swallowed, in Hollywood, more
meat. You got me through
long nights with your coal-scuttle
panic, don't be scared
to scream when it hurts
and oh mother it hurts, tonight
we are twenty-seven, we are
alone, you are dead.

Rooms in Bloomsbury

The horrors of the personal, revealed
in indiscreetly published *cahiers*,
lean on the pristine chronicle. "Today
A and Z used my room instead. I feel
nothing, although I saw them on the bed
one instant before switching off the light
again. Read Stendhal in the bath all night."
As, circumspectly in that epoch, Z
writes, ". . . then, at last, they published it, and for
the first time public notice shaped my life,
till world events intruded. Even C
could not ignore the change, and, as for me,
I soon displeased my publishers, my wife
and friends, enlisted and endured the War."

Aube Provençale

Absent, this morning
the cock crowed later than the nine o'clock
church bells. Cherry boughs
bronzed outside the casement,
and I woke

sweating, with my hands
between my thighs, from a dream
of archives, wanting you
under me, my breasts hollowed in the arc
below your ribs,

my knees between your knees,
my hands behind your ears, my cheek
furrowed in your chest, tasting
our mingled night sweat, tasting
your sleep.

I'll make a song
on your neck cords. Wake up,
bird asleep against my hipbone,
and crow, it's already
morning.

Crépuscule Provençale

Cursing the mistral,
the neighbor elbows doorward.
It batters on tiled roofs, whips cascades
across the hill face. Meet me
near the sea,

I wrote; come to me
through polyglot gossip,
and we'll share mountains, oceans, islands.
November is wind and rain
here. Heavy

persimmons, bloody
on black branches, gleamed in blue
afternoon, clear as a hidden valley.
Lapis beyond the green gorge, the sea spilled
its chalice

of hills. It's a month
since I left you, near water, wet
pebbles in our pockets, I'll write, our cheeks
brushed, salt gusts already
between us.

Dark now, shutters bang
stucco. Later I'll drink
by the fire, and let three tongues of
chatter silence an absence sung
in the wind.

Untoward Occurrence at
Embassy Poetry Reading

Thank you. Thank you very much. I'm pleased
to be here tonight. I seldom read
to such a varied audience. My poetry
is what it is. Graves, yes, said love, death
and the changing of the seasons
were the unique, the primordial subjects.

I'd like to talk about that. One subjects
oneself to art, not necessarily pleased
to be a colander for myths. It seasons
one to certain subjects. Not all. You can read
or formulate philosophies; your death
is still the kernel of your dawn sweats. Poetry

is interesting to people who write poetry.
Others are involved with other subjects.
Does the Ambassador consider death
on the same scale as you, Corporal? Please
stay seated. I've outreached myself. I read
your discomfort. But tonight the seasons

change. I've watched you, in town for the season,
nod to each other, nod to poetry
represented by me, and my colleagues, who read
to good assemblies; good citizens, good subjects
for gossip. You're the audience. Am I pleased
to frighten you? Yes and no. It scares me to death

to stand up here and talk about real death
while our green guerrillas hurry up the seasons.

They have disarmed the guards by now, I'm pleased
to say. The doors are locked. Great poetry
is not so histrionic, but our subjects
choose us, not otherwise. I will not read

manifestos. Tomorrow, foreigners will read
rumors in newspapers. . . . Oh, sir, your death
would be a tiresome journalistic subject,
so stay still till we're done. This is our season.
The building is surrounded. No more poetry
tonight. We are discussing, you'll be pleased

to know, the terms of your release. Please read
these leaflets. Not poetry. You're bored to death
with politics, but that's the season's subject.

A Christmas Crown

I

Son of the dark solstice descends the tree
into the winter city. Riversedge
receives him as the rusty currents dredge
our frozen offal heavily to sea.
Child of our Mother in the death of light,
torn out of blood onto a shattered mirror,
squall reasonable hungers to our terror;
it will not take so long tomorrow night.
The starry dragon will be drawn to scale,
exhaling central heating on the crib
or carton where the infant graingod breathes
and coughs up stringy gobbets on the wreaths,
decides to live; earth-warmed air swells his ribs
while she smiles at the moon, her plate, her pale.

II

While she smiles at the moon, her plate, her pale
reflection, tideridden ladylove
of corner boys and epileptics, of
remittance princes, alcoholics, frail
dexedrine beauties, we in lust of male
muses had best rededicate
postponed mornings. This time she might not wait.
In her thin arms the child begins to wail,
robust and greedy, sucking every sin
but hope out of her teeming hemisphere.
Will he rebuild our city where we stand
ritually dumbfounded by the hand
reflexes of any infant? Where
will he learn our hunger, and begin?

III

Will he learn our hunger and begin
the politic ascent? Our history
glyphs our bodies; querent to him we
flash autonomic broadcasts. On the skin
of a distracted shop girl: Monday's news,
produce of Sussex, a sermon on Greed.
I praise you, baby who still cannot read,
accept, acclaim, admonish, or accuse.
I have my woman's winter in my hands;
my mouth bleeds with a homeless appetite;
the several importunities of lust
grease my regard. In solitary trust,
I pledge infidel vigil as the night,
swollen with day birth, chills, cajoles, commands.

IV

Swollen with day, birth chills, cajoles, commands
simpler directions. We still want to go
back to the Good Place. We could finish grow-
ing up in an orderly, four-seasoned land-
scape, we tell each other, drinking gin-
and-limes on the terrace while the monster flock
moves through the hot rain to the western dock.
Here we are languid adolescents in
fiction, waiting for a Protagonist
to get us moving. Outside, the real snow
drifts to the real street. They've closed the bars,
and whiskey voices slide above the cars'
tarry andante, caroling her slow
pains as she brings her belly to the tryst.

V

Pain. As she brings her belly to the tryst,
invalids, children, and insomniacs
turn in their beds, wanting the daylight back;
and lovers, whose replenishment consists
of little sleeps between betraying dreams,
wake, thinking that blue window is another
blue window, and that heavy kiss is Mother's
send-off on a class hike in the Extremes.
More would be only fiction: how the dying,
the pious, the powerful, turn on their own
wheels of year-dark, emerge, or stay behind.
I don't know what the nursling in my mind
will grow to, only question an unknown
quality, voiced with a newborn's crying.

VI

Quality voiced with a newborn's crying,
impotent as an infant to reply
to questions or the chocolate-covered lie:
O wouldn't it be cozy to stop trying,
O give the music sheets, the cup, the child
back to the nice lady and come *on*
(who on the wet steps to the Underground
in Baker Street turned with jonquils and smiled).
When I have grown accustomed to the cold,
when I have grown accustomed to the dark,
the lean meat and the narrow bed, I will
not have accumulated virtue. Still
drifts feather the entrance to the park.
The birthday is eleven hours old.

VII

The birthday is eleven hours old.
The novelists' two sweet-stained daughters play
Camps under the kitchen stairs. Today,
hardly anything is bought or sold.
Hardly anybody eats alone.
Almost no trains run. Almost-suicides
and almost-murders lie in rows outside
the noisy quondam operating room
where an exhausted intern, twenty-three
years old, mops up and sews. The children sing
below our gossip. Roast and fruit and wine
and smoke mix in the air near dinnertime.
The guests file foodward while the darkening
sun of the dark solstice descends the tree.

F R O M

SEPARATIONS

1 9 7 6

The Callers

Pads in a quilted bathrobe to the door.
Today, she is a psychiatric nurse
tending the woman on the second floor
(chronic obesity) who has perverse
fantasies that lurk in corners, squat
beneath rouged lamps. Beyond the door are three
tall cutouts in the blinking sunlight that
stand forward as she clicks the peephole. She
pads in thermal quilting to the door,
counting the slap of mules from stair to stair,
as migraine repetitions lace her, bore
needle holes where her name escapes. Thick hair
like hers falls on the dark brow of one
boy whose hands hesitate toward her. A son
of hers, remembered with a cue
for swellings and excuses. Every year
brought the bloating and another new
wrinkled disappearance.
                              "Why are you here?
Your counselor should come this afternoon."
"I haven't had a counselor for years,
Mother."
          "Of course you have. He'll be here soon,"
and turns, and lets them follow her upstairs.

Squat in the reddened corners of the room,
shadows fidget in adrenal haze.
She keeps it twilight while the afternoon
light bars the window frames against the shades.
Hulking from the sofa, Walter stands
toward the ceiling, darkening the wall,

quakes and sits when they offer their hands
to him.
          "Walter, this is my son, Paul."
"I'm not Paul, Mother. I'm Thomas."
                              "Oh,
Thomas, your brother, Paul, is sick.
Sunday he was arrested. Do you know
Walter, my fiancé? It's so thick
in here, but I know I'll catch cold
if I open the windows," feels the chill
and tugs her sleeves down, wondering how old
he is now.
          "Raymond, Emmanuelle,
my mother."
              The man and woman near the door
come forward, smiling and severe.
New foster parents? What have they come for?
She wonders if they want to leave him here.
They shake her hand, sit in opposing chairs
in corners like good children washed for tea.
She licks her flaking lips and pats her hair.
"Thomas, why don't you ever write to me?
I'm working as a psychiatric nurse
you know, two afternoons a month.
I had a breakdown, you know. That's the curse
our family must live with. Everyone
has problems, that's what I always say.
Like my brother's drinking. Walter here
was my patient. He feels bad today.
We're getting married when he's well, next year.
No sense in rushing, is there, that's what I
always say, no sense."
                        The room is bright
enough to hurt her eyes.

                                   "Mother, why
was Paul arrested?"
                          "Last Saturday night
he stole ten dollars from a grocery store.
He works there afternoons, you know. He did it
for attention. I can't control him anymore.
He spent it all on candy. He admitted
he took it, to Miss Watson at the Home
he lives at. Sit there. Haven't I lost weight?"
They mustn't all look at her. Valium
calms them. Two fingers tap eight
palm doses.
                          Thomas squats on carpeting
in the fringed pool of a lamp, Emmanuelle
above him on a straight chair, fingering
the frayed cuffs of her suede jacket. Well
out of the light, blue-eyed Raymond cracks
his knuckles softly, softly, staring
at the line of Thomas's half-turned back.
Beside her, Walter's thick fingers are tearing,
crushing, rolling cellophane. She takes
the pack of cigarettes away. Today
she drops his dosage. Apprehension makes
a sweet taste in her mouth.
                                   "Now will you stay
in town awhile? How long have you been here?"
Darkness climbs the ladders on the wall,
menacing the ceiling. They appear
restive this evening. She must sweep out all
the corners. Thomas is a wicked boy
to run away from home. His mother takes
the kitchen knife and four pink pills today
for nerves. What is he saying? Her headache
is coming back. Inside the china cage

cracking behind her forehead, something blots
on the carpet. He was forward for his age.
Drips on porcelain forget-me-nots.
Compose the hands. "You know your grandmother
is dead. She went mad before she died.
She always asked for you. Always. Your brother
was away. You can't escape it, that's what I
always say. Last week your uncle called
but I hung up. That man is not allowed
in my house. My doctor says that alcohol
promotes mental decay. He said that now
I can treat myself, that's what he said,
write my own prescriptions."
                                    Walter prods
the sofa cushions with his fists and spreads
his knees.
            "Good health is a gift of God,"
and God will punish sinners. Thomas was
evil like her mother. They would talk
about her in the other room, play cards
and laugh.
            "I've got to go now." Walter works
his way up to an undetermined height
and tracks his shadow to the door.
                                    "Good-bye.
You'll come to dinner here on Sunday night."
He goes.
            "He's very sick, you know. He's my
patient."
            Thomas, near the woman's knee,
widens his dark eyes through vermilion shade.
"He's always been extremely kind to me.
Now we can talk, Thomas. You must stay
when Paul's counselor visits. Will you write

to Paul? I'm too nervous now, you know.
When Betty-Mae gives me my pills at night
she writes letters for me sometimes. Do you
remember Betty-Mae?" He nods his head
out of the puddled lamplight. Ashy dusk
fingers his smooth cheeks like, as if. Instead
of chicken, Betty-Mae could do a roast
on Sunday. Suddenly she feels
bloated, floating on her back in thick
sweet syrup. No cheating between meals,
the doctor said. Downstairs, somebody knocks.

Counting the careful steps down to the door,
she plucks the robe out over her belly. They
must not be left alone too long. One more
—what—she lost count of. But today
she is a psychiatric nurse. Her hands
realign the medication tray
to allow the doorknob. A brown man
with a brown briefcase and a gray
suit:
        "I'm from the Youth Board, ma'am.

                                Your son
is on my case file."
                Once again the blaze
of unfamiliar sky charring the dun
figure before it.
                "Well, come in."
                                She stays
fixed on the threshold, swaying with the street,
until he is above her on the stairs.
She turns, eyes full of ashes, with the sweet
taste in her mouth. Walking behind, she bears
herself as though her abdomen were big.

A nurse can't do that, though, because it looks
bad for the patients. She wonders if her legs
have swelled. Ahead, the Youth Board worker walks
into her parlor, passing Thomas where
he watches from the doorway.
                              "Hello, sir."
"Thomas, isn't it? What are you doing here?"
"This is my mother," standing next to her.
"Well, now you're out of our hands." Near the door,
Thomas hunkers on his heels again
between the strangers, as the counselor
walks to the couch. Pleasant to have nice men
for tea. "May I fix you some tea?"
"Thanks, I have other visits. I can't stay."
He opens up the briefcase on his knees.
"Our work comes first, that's what I always say."
He looks at her, and smiles as she sits down
beside him.
            "Your son is at La Honda Ranch
for Boys, about a half hour's drive from town.
If he does well there, he has a good chance
of coming home soon. I have photographs
to show you, of the building and the grounds.
They live better than we do, there."
                                    He laughs.
"One day you must come out and look around."
In a mottled cardboard frame like lace
are five pink stucco houses in a row,
each of whose door and windows make a face
like in a picture book her long-ago-
gone father gave her.
                      "Your boy will be in Section A
for six weeks, kept to grounds. In Section B
he can come to the city for the day
twice a month, on Sundays."

                               "Can I keep
the picture?"
                               "If he does well in Sec-
tion A, he goes to Section B
after six weeks. Otherwise, he is kept
in Section A. You can come to see
him, and the grounds, on any Sunday."
                                              "I
can't leave the house. I haven't been well. Now
I'm going back to work. I am a psy-
chiatric nurse, you know. How
is he doing? He's mentally ill,
you know."
                      "No, no one told me. . . ." Pad and pen
appear. "Mrs., uh, you'll have to tell
me about this."
                      "He's been sick since he was ten.
His records are with the Youth Guidance Board."
"I'm with the Board, ma'am, and I haven't seen
evidence . . ."
                      "My advice won't be ignored
as a professional."
                      "I haven't been
free to see your son. You may be right."
(At a gesture from Emmanuelle,
Raymond takes out cigarettes and lights
one for himself, for her, for Thomas.)
                                           "Will
you be able to provide a car
for the boy to come and visit you
on his free Sundays? In six weeks we are
transferring him to Section B where two
home visits monthly are permitted."
                                           "No,
I can't afford that. I don't drive.

My brother drives, but he is not allowed
in my house. When my mother was alive
she drove."
                    "I see. Well, perhaps you can call
another parent. I suppose you'd like to know
when Thomas will be coming home."
                                        "Paul,"
softly says Thomas from the carpet.
                                        "Oh,
yes. Paul."
           "He isn't coming here.
He never lived here. He was at a Home.
He was happy there. They know him there.
He should see a priest. He is a Ro-
man Catholic."
                 "I see." The ballpoint dips
as she picks up the eggshell cardboard stand,
traces pink houses under her fingertips
and presses it collapsed between her hands,
flat as a filing card. Paul is away,
and he will get a paper cup and pills
tonight at bedtime. Downstairs, Betty-Mae
is fixing supper. God the Father kills
the sinners' children. Thomas must not stay
past dark. Is it already dark?
The painted children rise outside.
                                   "Good day.
Call me if you have questions."
                               Is the mark
already on his forehead? Thomas rises
with the stranger.
                   "You should cut your hair,
Thomas."
         He blocks the lamp, revivifies

arachnid dark congealing under chairs.
They go out on the landing. Who will dance
in lapping spotlights on the street tonight?
Raymond looks toward the doorway, rubbing his hands.
Emmanuelle, smoking in the lamplight,
lifts her head and smiles. They both smile,
and Thomas insubstantially returns
like something that will move a little while
and then be still. This hunger, how it burns
under her heart. It's almost suppertime.
The three are standing, Thomas facing her,
a glowing shape on either side of him,
cutting scorched paths back to where they were
sitting. They can't come for her here. She lives
here. Everything went so well today.
She was a nurse. She'll tell them she forgives
Thomas . . .
          "Mother, we have to leave."
                                        They go away.

Alone, she tours around the room three times,
checking the placement of the figurines
and china cups. Behind the crystal chimes,
she finds the seven caps of Thorazine
she hid from Betty-Mae. Out of her sleeve,
she takes the picture of the Ranch for Boys
and sets it on the mantel. Streetlights weave
the wall. She draws the drapes to dull the noise.

Somewhere in a Turret

Somewhere in a turret in time,
castled and catacombed in but
still on a tan street that
ends with a blue-and-white gingerbread house,
those rooms are still filled
with our pictures and books. On the sill
our black-and-white cat hums after a fly.
It is getting light. When we come in,
no one will ask you to leave, no one will send me away.

Nobody lives in the present, time
has textures past and future that
tongues taste at, fingers feel for.
The present happens in rooms
I am not in; past rooms
are only momentarily
empty, if I knew how
to turn around, I would cross the threshold smiling.
No one would ask me to leave, no one would send me away.

Don't think I'm trying to ignore the time
I piled my things into a cab and left
a note for you and one for the dinner guests.
Those rooms have new tenants. You and I
may never share a closet or a towel rack
again. We contrived it. I am still
surprised waking up without you every morning.
But I can't camp out in your house or you in mine.
People would ask me to leave. People would send you away.

Still, I am an optimist. Sometime
we may be sitting, maybe near the ocean
on a cliff, and under the blown spray
get tangled in each other's fingers and hair;
and in that arbitrary future, your mouth
and the sea will taste of each other.
It is so easy to make things happen
like a freeze shot ending a movie
so you don't leave, and I don't go away.

But you know about words. You have had time
to figure out that hardly anyone
came back to bed because of a poem.
Poems praise and protect us from
our lovers. While I write this
I am not having heartburn
about your indifference. We could walk
into any room.
You wouldn't ask me to leave. I wouldn't send you away.

from Separations

I

Satisfied lovers eat big breakfasts. I
want black coffee and a cigarette
to dull this cottonmouth. Nine-ten. The wet-
faced construction workers hunkered by
the Pioneer Grill grin as I walk past.
You tried to be sleeping when I left
your room. The sweaty blanket hugged the cleft
between your buttocks. Now a crowd of fast
clouds scutters across the cautious sky
above the Fillmore West. We didn't make
it this time. Maybe it will take
another year. If you still want to try.
We try, and fail again, and try, and fail.
I'll be back home an hour before the mail.

V

This is a high and sprawling wooden flat
with seven rooms, three tenants, and four beds.
We all nurture each other in our heads
and keep our distances outside of that.
Each cares for his own plants and his own cat;
we all like gossip, magic, plots and food
and spending half a day on last night's mood
or conversation or delicious brat.
We all are vague with anger and affection.
I love them both, and not for power or sex,
and if they love me I am fortunate,
and if they love each other they'll debate
themselves; but we have saved each other's necks
for risking in more challenging directions.

VI

I still balk at my preference for rhyme
which hounds me like an inarticulate
and homely lover whom I wish would wait
outside; no, he can meet my friends this time,
screw vanity, I love him, he's my own
obsession. Voice: you clever girls and boys
may hear a kid stomping and making noise
because she's scared left in the house alone.
I set the midnight table for a new
unfledged muse, my dream-wounded animus
whose boots scuff up the stairs now. Angular
child, I have to tell them who you are,
and love you so much they will envy us
and want you so much they will want you too.

VII

I'll dabble in specifics in my bath,
fingering soap and dirt off pinkened skin.
"Someday when I'm notorious and thin,
supple in love, magnificent in wrath . . ."
Someday when I'm a lady nearing thirty,
who diets and has not had sex for weeks,
acne and crow's-feet fighting for my cheeks,
I'll wish my mind, and not my feet, were dirty.
I lean back in the tub, but now it's not
hot enough. I scrub my soles, and wish
Manhattan midnight steamed outside, and I
could go out coatless while the smoggy sky
simmered a river dawn of oil and fish
to take a walk with you. I can't. Now what?

IX

Most circumspect good friend, if, by "deceive,"
you mean keep secret who is in his bed,
trust that name, age, et cetera, were said
collect over Long Distance. I believe
in Higher Gossip, shifting states of soul
revealed in nervous tics, beer and bons mots:
what do you think he thinks, I want to know,
and feels, and is maintaining in control.
And I am fairly confident that he
would also want to know that sort of thing,
at the most cynical, because he craves
reassurance I still misbehave.
O Doubtful Thomas, stop malingering
and tell me what he's saying about me!

XIV

Friend (this is an imaginary letter
to someone I don't know), out of the hewn-
rock mountains, with the muddy morning rain
raising steam on spring pools (but a scatter
of snowfields on the peaks), the train descends
to prairies looking shabby under storm
blankets. I am eating bread and cheese
to stretch two dollars out over three days.
(Vancouver was extravagant.) I'm warm
jackknifed under my fur. The train's growl blends
with nightsounds of old men, babies, a plains-
woman's beery laugh. Legs cramped, I go
to sleep, rocked by a Cree kid's radio
wailing blues' soulsolace on the night train.

XVI

Culled from the brambled ceiling of my wide-
eyed latternights, he spends the afternoon
across the room, quiet at first, but soon
proffering novels about suicide
and madness in instructional detail.
This is the way it's done. Watch every crack
in the soiled wall flap open and coax back
your eyes to where I stand, a limber, pale
absence. Dead woman, you are not my twin;
why do we have a brother, following
me to foreign cities, saying: make
words, make noise, make time, tonight you'll wake
staring in half-light, sweating, lingering
under my cold suggestions on your skin.

XVIII

A February of the merely real,
plumbers, not bayonets, outside the door,
colds, personal despair. I wrote, "The war
is far away," back to Perine Place reel-
ing and sick with tear gas from a taut
poets-cum-journalists' soirée. The shades
were drawn. We joked about the barricades,
listening to gunfire. I got caught
by a bugmask's canister on Haight.
Sinecured exiles with unfunny eyes
converge on the Cultural Attaché's
free whiskey, playing Corner Points for praise.
It's hard to tell the poets from the spies.
The war is far away. Will wait. Will wait.

Rhetoric

Friend, then, whatever has become of us
since each for each was the anonymous
stranger whose elusive qualities
as Other in the Dialogue more civilized
poets apostrophize?

Foundered on languages,
discovering each was another whose
perceived uncipherable difference frees
or limits, to get this far, just this far,
we have become precisely what we are.

Villanelle: Late Summer

I love you and it makes me rather dull
when everyone is voluble and gay.
The conversation hits a certain lull.

I moon, rattled as china in a bull
shop, wanting to go, wanting to stay.
I love you and it makes me rather dull.

You might think I had cotton in my skull.
And why is one in Staithes and not in Hay?
The conversation hits a certain lull.

You took a fretful, unoriginal
and unrelaxing friend on holiday.
I love you and it makes me rather dull.

A sheepish sky, with puffs of yellow wool,
watches the tide interrogate the bay.
The conversation hits a certain lull.

And I am grimly silent, swollen full
of unsaid things. I certainly can't say
"I love you." And it makes me rather dull.
The conversation hits a certain lull.

The Companion

Everywhere you are coaxing the mad
boy into your room. You offer him
cold meat and beer. You light the fire
or the stove or the electric grate.
It is always cold. The winter city
solidifies under pale sun. The street
is full of little knots of gossiping
men. He crouches on your narrow bed,
cracking his knuckles in his lap. His hair
is dirty, falling in his eyes. His eyes
are muddy, fixed on you. You sit
cross-legged on the floor next to the grate,
chain-smoking, eating a yellow pear
down to the core. It is all gone. What will
you say to him? He has nothing to say
to you, staring at his large red hands. He is
not real. His baggy olive corduroys
are frayed through at the knees. You watch his knees
for some fraternal gesture. Now your face
is sweating. Every pore glistens with oil.
His cheeks are pocked. He knows about your dream.
There is nothing he can tell you, but you watch
his arms, his tense neck, scrawl an alphabet
older than birds' teeth on the patchy wall.
He is evidently used to ladies
alone in patchy rooms, used to ladies
who come home from work and staple tapestries
no one will ever see on the blue ceiling
above the bed, used to ladies
with plants, cats, paintings, Gordon's gin and pills.

He has no double. Objects come in pairs:
shoes, lamps, gloves, couples dining at tables
for two, policemen, telephone repairmen, nuns,
sailors on leave. But you and he are no
pair. Peach stone of solitude, he is
cracking his knuckles in your head, suggesting
only what you told him, drinking your beer,
eating your words, eating your sweaty hours,
bargaining eyes for time, trading his pain
for your sleep, all without a word
you can remember. You will look for words
in his ears, under his chewed nails, between his livid,
thin shanks. You will look for words
accrued behind the posters on the wall,
clogging the sink drain, in the frying pan
sticky with last night's curry, in a glass,
an ashtray, a green sock under the bed.
Objects crawl with words, rupture their pairs,
pile up between you. He gets easily
drunk. You too. You are my family
after all, pouring on the gin,
little brother, enigmatic cousin,
mother's sky-blue boy. Must every lover
leave you here, demanding plastic screen
of what an everyday good lady wants?
No lover, though, no novel, no landscape
intimating frenzy. Curtains and walls.
He leaves. Next morning you are on a train
nearing the sea. Rose dawn beyond Marseilles
and 5 A.M. awakenings are normal
on trains. Perhaps it was his dream
you forgot this morning; vision of
your mind, a cheesecloth or a tea strainer
that nightmares filter through. Midnight gut pain,

cold tiles, boots, darkness, to the john next door,
then lying in the morning garden, under
a cherry tree, faint whining of a loom
inside the house, a leather-cheeked old man
with a blue beret, hunching for violets
in the next field. I tricked you, Little Brother,
enclosed you in my belly. I will not
produce you here. Little Brother
waits after dinner in the outlanders'
café, drinking a marc and Schweppes,
looking like that Austrian émigré
with the peculiar eyes. You leave your friends
stroking each other's knees and gossiping,
to sit with him. He still has nothing
to say. The thick white saucers
pile up. You lean against the heater.
Last Saturday, one hundred forty-seven
adolescents burned to death, clawing the nailed-
shut fire exit of a thé dansant:
Grenoble. The kids shout in the room next door,
drinking beer and roasting chestnuts, dancing
badly. They have the elegant thin bones
of Leonardo angels, last year's slang.
Most of them are fourteen. Little Brother
is hitchhiking to Carcassonne. One boy,
pale as a mushroom thinking a blond mustache,
rests his clubbed right foot in a workhorse boot,
reversed, against the bar rail, watching.
What makes you think a cripple ought to know
any better. Sentimental bitch.
And goes, and you rejoin your friends. You wish
your train would come. Tomorrow your train comes.
You wish some enterprising sorcerer
would save a niche in his pentangular

observatory for you. Angular
and shy in the muse's naked outfit, he
enfolds you in the corporeal star
where Little Brother, scarlet in your head
and smug, still can't prank swords into your bed.
The train curves up abruptly from the sea
and you veer up from your unlikely wish
into a windowful of scenery.
I'll bring the loaves, my old. You'll fry the fish.
It's L. B. come to keep you company.
Was that your pincushion under the seat
last night? Silent before, now garrulous;
you wish he'd shut his face and put his feet
down. Mais quelle gueule! Built like a bus
you are, and with a face like runny cheese
this morning. Pitiful. Cat got your sleep?
The Dijonnais truck salesman plants his knees
on either side of yours, leans forward. Keep
two conversations going, c'est pas chouette.
You could do without both, and watch the rilled
blade of the Rhone cut valleys. Etiquette:
answer, smile, don't throw things. Have you killed
your mother yet? Boys weaned on paradox
bore me. Go away. He goes away,
leaving the commerçant in purple socks
leering. He's kept that leer on since Marseilles.
He left you alone in Venice. Silent,
as the gray water slurped the dirty white
carved landings, you rode the vaporetto like
other tourists, watching the hollow stage-
set city retreat to Tintoretto's age,
or Byron's, more nostalgic, less remote.
Scummed winter water nibbled on the boat
shoring at the Ferrovia where you

present yourself again at almost dawn
for drizzling Florence in the afternoon.
Now, in another room, you see yourself
putting a bowl of milk beside the door,
hanging up garlic from the molding, learning
Greek. You could be crouching by the fire
with an unopened book, again redoing
your last spoiled scene, washing your hair again,
washing the dishes, washing your face, bemused in
your own bad smell. Instead you set
a pint of bitter and some sandwiches
out on the coffee table with your borrowed
typewriter. Everywhere you are
coaxing him into your room.

The Last Time

Somebody has endlessly postponed
this summer; it is chilly and uncertain
as you, my own, not in the least my own.
I watched clouds move through the organza curtain
all afternoon. The noises of the farm
and loud birds ravaging Tom's kitchen garden
break on my book. Untrustworthy, the light
shifts every hour, wind sun fog sun wind storm.
I can't blame you, or ask your pardon,
or dream the day into another night

and wake up foundering between self-pity
and despair, the way I did today,
and take a morning train back to the city
where nothing much will happen anyway,
dubious individuals will write
dubious poetry, children will get cuffed
for nothing, and not forget it, I will fault
everyone fastidiously, tight-
assed and skeptical, obscure enough
to get away with it. O could I halt

this headfirst fall and rest love in your green
approval, tasting you like certainty,
summer would certainly start, something clean
and mobile as hill winds would move with me
and I would do . . . No, I do not believe
any of this, invoke it when I fear
the dull immobile speechless bland inert
mad lady who sits in me when I leave,

comfy as anything. Through her queer
nerveless hide, nothing pleasures, nothing hurts,

she could sit in the same place all day, all day,
not seeing, not hearing, not deaf, not blind,
her eyes like marbles and her flanks like whey;
the Sow reposes sated on my mind,
sated on what would have been a clean
if bitter lyric, setting me apart
from people who can say "I did," "I thought,"
as real things. I have said what I mean,
more than I meant; and if I start
over, from the beginning, if she bought

my silence with that other fear: you will
always be alone, I will console
you, I would have to be still
or tell lies, if I believed in a soul,
damn it, if I believed in my art, fake
it. And I will believe in that,
if necessary, as an act of will,
and she, stuporous lunatic, makes me make
poems; more than love or fame, her flat
face presses inside my face; she spills

through me, hypoglycemic languor
paralyzing rage, her rage, my rage.
Poles: pain and insensibility, anger
and absence, the senile queen, the murdering page.
He keeps me up all night. She makes me sleep
all day. Now clogged and vague, I maul the pain
to shape. They'll never let me out. Or I'm
not going. Anyway, not off the deep
end. Lovely people, I won't come again.
This is the last time. (That was the last time.)

After the Revolution

There are different ways of dying without
actually dying. I was nineteen.
So was Milo. Pavel was twenty-two. The square
was hotter than this beach; the no-man's-land
between July and October
when anything can happen
                        and nothing does.
They searched me. Nothing. They left me behind.
Every touch threatened; not the way a boy's
skin tingles to be touched.
                      If the gift leaves?
Might as well die.
                I woke up with that line
and a bad temper. We waited
to see them on those balconies
as if they were girls.
                I hardly know you:
an approximate age, oiled skin,
stones in the sun. We smelled each other.
Fear, yes. And, then, they had touched me.
So we waited. Are you a journalist?
I hope not. Why does it come down to
language? Pressures of bright air
over that other city; incipient autumn
swelled red and yellow skins. An instrument
incises the rough bark (feel it
signaling in the palm's crutch); thick sap
oozes amber marbled cream, the instant's
crystal, for the cabinet, crammed
with history. There are
unchronicled moments, the plane tree

knifed on the air in the square court.
The boys waited.
                        We waited.
                                    Dear friend; I am trying
to organize my expedition toward
the source.
                        Every bedizened traveler
retailing gossip in the Market with
chunks of dark amber, angels enameled on tin,
makes me think I can discover, if not
the actual "lake between three purple mountains"
above the falls, at least some old bachelor
with odd tastes, some witch's brat daughter,
who has been there, or claims it, and will show
(but not sell) a pebble, a dried herb
that smells like copper and quince. . . . If I do not
come back, if I disprove your theory
in a large-circulation periodical
or anything equally tasteless, remember
this note, and the token
I enclose.
                        I will not be able
to lunch with you on Saturday.
                                    Sincerely,
Dear friend:
                        Perhaps you will understand
when I say, I can no longer tolerate
this city. . . . No . . . The two young nuns
whom we watched strolling in the cloister
through the gap in the wall . . . if I said, their gait
seemed peculiar; if I added
the ostensible boy-poet lodged
in what was Mother's room has got a pattern
to his intensities . . . I will not be

drawn into events that I cannot
control or understand. These things concern
soldiers, economists, geographers,
but I will not be made historical
by chance. Good-bye. Perhaps you know
more of this than I do, have considered
the possibility of my . . . retreat.
I must miss you on Saturday.
                              Yours faithfully,
Read it back. Tell me what I said.
                              Words.
The body's heavy syllables. Touch me.
Say. Nerves said, You will begin
to finish dying. The children are running away.
They are hiding in the gorse bushes. They
dribble your inner thigh. They are throwing
chocolate wrappers from the balcony.
What are they whispering? Tell me.
                              Milo remembered
a child on the beach, a fox-faced little girl
carving something from driftwood. It was late August,
early evening. He was nineteen. He gave her
half his cheese and two tomatoes. She was carving
an old woman in a shawl. Cheese brine
on her fingers stained the dry wood. Her hair
was cropped against lice, gold stubble on her neck.
I thought of touching her there. It was not
Milo, it was I. The salt still on her mouth.
Pavel had a stolen rifle. Milo
had an American pistol. You are not
a journalist?
                              I'm almost twelve,
she said. I already have breasts.
I can read French. I read *Madame Bovary*.

If they fire into the crowd, I said. I thought,
Pavel would be a handsome grandfather.
We are playing stupid games. I will kiss you, I said,
but I'll never speak to you again
if you tell anyone.
                    It flowered
his sweaty shirt front. He crumpled, quizzically,
into the dazed heat. *"Pavel!"*
They searched me. Nothing. They left me behind.
A red ball sun plumbed the translucent water.
She lay on top of me, her knees
rubbing my trunks, her cotton shirt
damp and gritty on my bare chest. Licked salt
off my lips.
                I looked for Milo for three days.
Dear friend:
                    It was once my language; now I can
barely read it. Even this note
may be written in code.
                            Yours in haste,
Here comes Pavel with lunch. The children
went crabbing with Milo and Douina. Don't
say anything to Milo . . . his job . . .
you understand. Not
as one might have wished.

Geographer

for Link (Luther Thomas Cupp), 1947–1974

I

I have nothing to give you but these days,
laying broken stones on your waste, your death.
(The teeth behind kisses.) Nothing rhymes with death.
Richter plays Bach. My baby daughter plays
with a Gauloise pack. Once I learned pain and praise
of that good body, that mouth you curved for death.
Then your teeth clenched. Then you shivered. Seeing death.
Another of those mediocre lays.
Little Brother, of all the wastes, the ways
to live a bad movie, work a plot to death.
You worked your myth to death: your real death.
I've put my child to bed. I cannot eat.
This death is on my hands. This meat dead meat.

II

There is a cure for love. It is absence. There is a cure
for grief. (It is absence.) I cannot say,
you died, and I don't want to live today.
I fed my child. I learned to drive a car.
I went to work. The baby is in bed.
This is a formula I used before.
(I ate a veal chop.) Word, word, word: the cure
for hard nights. Somebody was always dead,
but not, certainly, you. You rattled speed-
ing, seven-thirty, through the door,
awash with daffodils. Did I stay
up all night drawing the bowl of fruit? I did.
And then we went to bed and slept till four.
You kept the drawing when I went away.

III

Sorry, I can't make any metaphors.
There is no talking horse. Billy the Kid
did what he did, and he died. Death is no mid-
wife birthing you to myth. You died, that's yours;
death is nobody, death is a word,
dying happens. People die. I will die.
You are dead, after five minutes of dy-
ing. Were you afraid? Last night I heard
of another poet dead, by her own hand,
it seems (oh, how I wish there were more
boozy women poets, aged sixty-seven:
new book, new man, wit and kitchen noted for
flavor). *If there's a Rock 'n' Roll Heaven*
They sure have a Hell of a band.

IV

Metaphor slid in on the radio
like vision's limit; we see the night sky
a planetarium dome; mind, or eye,
won't take starry infinity, won't know
for more than a dawning shudder: I will die.
You died. Once, we walked along the beach
in the Pacific autumn twilight. Reach-
ing for something, knowing you and not knowing, I
asked, were you afraid of dying. "No,
I don't know." I wanted to say how, ly-
ing in bed, I was ten, in the swish of cars
through rain outside, I knew, what you knew, and know
nothing now, that I was going to die,
and howled, hurled into the enormous stars.

V

This is for your body hidden in words
in the real city and the invisible city:
your words, Jack's, Hunce's, Lew's, Gerry's, my words,
golden scarabs, a carapace of words
crystaled opaque over your eyes, this death
that was your eyes. Hating words, I fumble words
into a bridge, a path, a wall. My words
are not to coax your saltiness this time;
they freeze you in this agate slice of time
where you would not be now except for words.
I am thirty-two. I have a child.
You were twenty-six, never a child

never a grown-up. At my feet, my child
puts a box in a bigger box, babbling almost-words.
You were eighteen, a smooth-cheeked, burning child,
black and gold on the snow where terrible chil-
dren honed the facets of the winter city.
I was twenty-three. I let you be the child.
Last century, I would have died in child-
birth, proving nothing at all in my death
except that women were duped, even to death.
I love my loud brave dirty woman-child.
She and I have gotten through, this time.
And you snuffed yourself out at the same time.

Bright in a frieze, the figures whittled of time
rescued from love and money, friends and child:
gem-lit bodies locked under my fur (near time
the Museum closed), we writhed, reflected; the time
we howled and rolled all night, elbows and words

gasping absurd (to get to work on time
we slept, at last, feet to head); the time
we mapped an imaginary city
on your graph pad. Shanghai, Leningrad, what cities
we pored over in picture books, marking time!
Trite, how a lithe boy giving the slip to death
skips over maps, and one slip is, anyway, death.

Now I will be face-to-face with death
which has no face. I have had two weeks' time
to heft and weigh and hold and swallow your death.
I have written a lot of lines that end with *death*.
I have held your death the way I hold my child,
but it has no weight and it has no voice. The death
of a red begonia from frost, the hibernal death
of the Heath horse chestnuts, colored, odored words
pile up. But I have not found the words
to thread the invisible waste of your death;
the quicksilver veins threading the map of a city,
till the lights all froze out, all over the city.

I am alive, in a gray, large, soft-edged city
you never saw, thinking of your death
in what is an imaginary city
for me. Once, I imagined a city.
You were born there. You took me there. In time
somebody might have thought it was my city.
Night after day after night, I mapped the city
on the brown geography of its child;
and the cliffs and hills and gemmed sky charted the child
like a wound flowering the streets of the city.
The wound clotted with jewels. The jewels were words.
I left you in the city, and took away words.

From the gutted building, we salvaged words,
raced down Nob Hill at midnight, bad child, bad child,
thinking we'd gotten away with it that time.
Past one now, and the night contains your death.
Now you have visited too many cities.

F R O M

TAKING NOTICE

1 9 8 0

Feeling and Form

for Sandy Moore and for Susanne K. Langer

Dear San: Everybody doesn't write poetry.
A lot of people doodle profiles, write
something they think approximates poetry
because nobody taught them to read poetry.
Rhyming or trailing gerunds, clumps of words
straggle a page, unjustified—poetry?
It's not like talking, so it must be poetry.
Before they learn to write, all children draw
pictures grown-ups teach them how not to draw.
Anyone learns/unlearns the craft of poetry
too. The fourth grader who gets a neat like-
ness of Mom in crayon's not unlike

the woman who sent you her Tone Poem, who'd like
her admiration praised. That isn't poetry,
unless she did the work that makes it like
this, any, work, in outrage, love, or lik-
ing an apple's October texture. Write
about anything—I wish I could. It's like
the still lives you love: you don't have to like
apples to like Cézanne. I do like words,
which is why I make things out of words
and listen to their hints, resounding like
skipping stones radiating circles, draw-
ing context from text, the way I've watched you draw

a pepper shaker on a table, draw
it again, once more, until it isn't like

anything but your idea of a draw-
ing, like an idea of movement, draw-
ing its shape from sequence. You write poetry.
I was a clever child who liked to draw,
and did it well, but when I watch you draw,
you rubber-face like I do when I write:
chewed lip, cat-tongue, smiles, scowls that go with right
choices, perplexed, deliberate, withdrawn
in worked play, conscious of the spaces words
or lines make as you make them, without words

for instant exegesis. Molding words
around a shape's analogous to draw-
ing these coffee cups in settings words
describe, but whose significance leaves words
unsaid, because it's drawn, because it's like
not my blue mug, but inked lines. Chosen words
—I couldn't write *your white mug*—collect words
they're meant, or drawn to, make mental space poetry
extends beyond the page. If you thought poetry
was merely nicely ordered private words
for two eyes only, why would you say, "Write
me a letter, damn it!" This is a letter, right?

Wrong. Form intimates fiction. I could write
me as a mathematician, weave in words
implying *you* a man, sixteen, a right-
handed abstract expressionist. I'd write
untruths, from which some other *you* could draw
odd inferences. Though I don't, I write
you, and you're the Donor on the right-
hand panel, kneeling in sable kirtle. Like-
ly I'm the lady left of you, who'd like

to peer into your missal, where the writ-
ing (legible Gothic) lauds in Latin poetry
the Lady at the center. Call her poetry,

virtual space, or Bona Dea. Poetry
dovetails contradictions. If I write
a private *you* a public discourse, words
tempered and stroked will draw you where you draw
these lines, and yours, convergent, made, unlike;

that likelihood draws words I write to poetry.

The Regent's Park Sonnets

I

"That was in another country," but the wench
is not yet dead, parks the red-striped pushchair
near the Rose Garden and turns loose her fair
Black Jewish Woman Baby; picks a bench
scoured by warm winds; (five years ago, twelve days
and nights, another country, where the might-
be was incarnated every night),
squints, focusing on the child, not yours, who plays
explorers. You are in another count-
ry, houseguesting, annual August rounds
as solid as ripe apples, on the grounds
of continuity, convenience (*Con!*
suggests itself; it seems I can't be hon-
est and not too bitter or too blunt).

II

You rang me up this morning from Marseilles
echoing other lines and other lives.
The best-intentioned women sound like wives
sometimes: why couldn't I find something to say
but "When will you be back?" Above the play-
ground, like a capsuled world, a plane
heads, fortunately, north. Fresh after rain
the sky is innocently blue. Away
from frisking kids, including mine, I write
stretched on a handkerchief of pungent dry
grass, wishing I could take off my shirt.
I word old wounds. As usual, they hurt
less. Iva's giving someone's bike a try.
We could be on a plane tomorrow night.

III

Some table talk at lunch, of memory:
the anecdotal hypnotist who could
unlock the nursery. Not babyhood
occurred to me, but two weeks buried by
the next five years. That's when I should have made
poems each extraordinary day
and I could read them now and brush away
the dust accrued over a half decade,
and I'd remember everything we said
when I thought we were saying everything.
We did, I guess, what everybody does,
if I were better at remembering.
Sometimes I wonder who I thought I was
and who on earth I thought was in my bed.

IV

"What's in a park they warn girls out of?" "Queers."
That's what I thought of parks at seventeen:
hunting grounds, pleasure gardens, never seen
by day eyes, girls' eyes, blinkered eyes like theirs—
the clucking mums on benches near the swings.
I've joined their number after fifteen years.
I'm sure behind the bushes after hours
all sorts of lewd and fascinating things
still happen. But they won't happen to me.
If I were tall and tan and twenty-three,
I still would be a woman. So I stay
among women and children, on the day
side, guarding a blue pail and red spade.
I wonder how they manage to get laid?

V

One master, aged, as I am, thirty-two,
all summer sonneted adulterous
love: cocktails and woods, fortuitous
meetings, public words that no one knew
were private. This playground is an odd land-
scape for longings in an afternoon
splashed with babies' bright clothes. Near six now. Soon,
grown tired of high adventure in the sand-
pit, we will head for home and food.
We—you and I—don't have a thing to hide.
We need not meet through pseudonyms and gin.
Yet there's no common space for meeting in,
and secrets fence me in on every side.
This week is taking longer than it should.

VI

Another poet, woman and alive,
recalls: sorrow is politics. Another
woman, not my tormentor, not my mother,
waits for you, in a castle. Gosh! We thrive,
it seems, on *Woman's Own*. On women's own
solitude, uncertainty, old fears
nursed, like a taste for brandy, over years.
"If you don't mind, I'd still rather not know
you." Wound like clockwork, she and I,
speechless, oppose. Central, you stroke one, strike
the other. In New York, I lived with two
men; we loved each other. Do you *like*
either? Replaceable, we know it, sigh,
resigned, while options preen in front of you.

VII

Thursday, the eighth of August, four o'clock.
Fire-salvaged wood desk filled the window bay,
notebook, cat curled round coleus: the way
I spent those afternoons. Downstairs, a knock.
Midnight at the Savoy-Tivoli
still talking; me guilty you paid the bill
while I was in the john. Bar, home, alone, still
dazed. Paul and Bill: "Have you noticed he's
most attractive?" "Oh, shut up!" Ninety-one
degrees today, in London. On the dock
flushed kids queue for canoes. Iva, in bright
blue shorts, clambers the bench. On Friday night
hands brushed in the dark, stayed: finished, begun.
—Friday, the eighth of August, four o'clock.

VIII

Gino's hummed an epithalamium:
one resident fag hag and pedophile
reformed! You knocked Jack Daniel's back in style.
In two days you would go and fetch your son.
Meanwhile bought rounds. I think groped Nemi's knee.
I almost minded. Under the table, gripped
my legs in yours. "Let's go." My cronies quipped
farewells. (The pub downstairs, less leisurely,
disgorges footsteps and unsteady songs
bracketed by cars.) Late through the long
night, our tongues grappled in a double cave.
Naked swimmers plunged in wave over wave,
hands, mouths, loins, filling and filled, until we gave
ourselves back, tired, seawashed and salty, strong.

Coda

It was not my mother or my daughter
who did me in. Women have been betrayed
by history, which ignores us, which we made
like anyone, with work and words, slaughter
and silver. "The Celts treated their women well . . ."
(I guess their wives were Picts.) A man at a table—
like you, whose face is etched on my nights, unable
to see as I see that first face first in hell-
ish uncertainties, and then unlearn, relearn.
The peach-faced Cypriot boy brings us more wine.
Cryptic, perhaps, yes, as this hedged return.
I choke up, as if I had breathed water.
Other, not polar, not my mother or daughter.
Some woman might have understood the line.

Living in the Moment

This is a seasick way,
this almost/never touching, this
drawing-off, this to-and-fro.

Adrienne Rich, "The Demon Lover"

Two blue glasses of neat
whiskey, epoxy-mended Japanese
ashtray accruing Marlboro and Gauloise
butts, umber and Prussian blue ceramic cups
of Zabar's French Roast, cooling. You acquired
a paunch; I am almost skinny
as I'd like to be. You are probably
right, leaving. We've been here
thousands of miles away, hundreds of times before.

I try to be a woman I could love.
I am probably wrong, asking
you to stay. Blue cotton jersey
turtleneck, navy corduroy Levi's,
nylon briefs, boy's undershirt, socks, hiking shoes:
inside (bagged opals, red silk swaddles a
Swiss Army knife) a body nobody sees.
Outside, cars and men screech on Amsterdam Avenue
hundreds of times, before, thousands of miles away,

hidden in cropped hair like a lampshade,
I try to say what I think I mean.
My thirty-five-year-old white skin wants you
to stroke back twenty-seven-year-old certainty
I'd better doubt. The time's stopped
light hours ago on the smelly East River

glazes my eyes with numbers, years. We both
wear glasses. We both have children
thousands of miles away. Hundreds of times before,

we agree, the nerves' text tricked us
to bad translation. My wrapped sex cups
strong drink. A woman honed words
for this at an oak desk above the Hudson
River in November; cross-legged on woven straw
in a white room in a stucco house; locked
in the bathroom away from the babies, notebook
on her knees. I repeat what we were asking
hundreds of times before. Thousands of miles away,

I am leaving you at Heathrow. Revolution
of a dozen engines drowns parting
words, ways: "I should be asking you to stay."
I shouldn't be asking you to stay. We finish
our courage. Tumblers click on the table.
Tumblers click in the lock. I unwrap
cotton and corduroy, nylon and cotton,
wrap up in flannel for the night that started
thousands of miles before, hundreds of times away.

Adult Entertainment

Agreed: Familiarity breeds
confusion; cautious consistency is better.
You would be harried; I (and she) be hurt.
Sane speaking distance is safest and best.

Under an academic tweed
jacket, over a secondhand Shetland sweater,
a cotton jersey and an undershirt,
your naked hand welcomes my naked breast.

Prayer for My Daughter

You'll be
coming home alone on the AA
Local from Canal Street, 1 A.M.
Two Black girls, sixteen, bushy
in plaid wool jackets, fiddle
with a huge transistor radio.
A stout bespectacled white woman reads
Novy Mir
poking at a gray braid.
A thin blue blonde dozes on shopping bags.
Tobacco-colored, hatchet-faced and square,
another mumbles in her leather collar.
Three sharp Latinas jive round the center post, bouncing
a pigtailed baby, tiny sparkling
earrings, tiny work overalls.
A scrubbed corduroy girl wearing a slide rule eyes
a Broadway redhead wearing green fingernails.
A huge-breasted drunk, vines
splayed on cheeks, inventively
slangs the bored brown
woman in a cop suit, strolling.
You'll get out at 81st Street (Planetarium)
and lope upstairs, traveling light-years.
The war is over!

1976

The bathroom tiles are very pink and new.
Out the window, a sixty-foot willow
tree forks, droops. Planted eighteen years ago,
its huge roots choke the drains. The very blue
sky is impenetrable. I hear you
whine outside the locked door. You're going to cry.
If I open the door, I'll slap you. I've
hit you six times this morning. I threw
you on the rug and smacked your bottom. Slapped
your face. Slapped your hands. I sit on the floor.
We're both scared. I picked you up, held you, lov-
ing your cheek's curve. Yelled, shook you. I want to stop
this day. I cringe on the warm pink tiles of
a strange house. We cry on both sides of the door.

Third Snowfall

Take with you also my curly-headed four-year-old child.
Josephine Miles, "Ten Dreamers in a Motel"

Another storm, another blizzard
soaks the shanks and chills the gizzard.
Indoors, volumed to try a Stoic, a
four-year-old plays the *Eroica*
three times through. Young Ludwig's ears?
No, only an engineer's
delight in Running the Machine.
Pop! Silence? "I was just seein'
if I could make the tape run back."
"Don't." "If the knob is on eight-track
and I put on a record, what
happens? . . . It's turning, but it's not
playing." "That's what happens." "Oh.
Which dial is for the radio?
I'm going to jump up on your back!
Swing me around!" A subtle *crack*
and not-so-subtle knives-in-spine.
"Get down, my back's gone out! Don't whine
about it, I'm the one that's hurt."
"I'm sorry . . . Did I have dessert?
What's water made of? Can it melt?"
(I know how Clytemnestra felt.)
"I want a cookie. What is Greek?
Will I be taller by next week?
Is this the way a vampire growls?
I'm going to dress up in the towels.
Look! I can slide on them like skis!
Hey, I've got dried glue on my knees.

Hey, where are people from? The *first*
ones, I mean. What was the Worst
Thing You Ever Ate?" *Past* eight
at last, I see. "Iva, it's late."
"It's not. I want some jam on bread."
"One slice, then get your ass in bed."
"No, wait until my record's over.
I want my doll. And the Land-Rover
for Adventure People. Mom, are
you *listening*? Where's the doll's pajamas?
There's glue or something in my hair.
Can I sleep in my underwear?
I think I need the toy firefighter
guy too . . . I'm thirsty . . ." *und so weiter.*

Iva's Pantoum

We pace each other for a long time.
I packed my anger with the beef jerky.
You are the baby on the mountain. I am
in a cold stream where I led you.

I packed my anger with the beef jerky.
You are the woman sticking her tongue out
in a cold stream where I led you.
You are the woman with springwater palms.

You are the woman sticking her tongue out.
I am the woman who matches sounds.
You are the woman with springwater palms.
I am the woman who copies.

You are the woman who matches sounds.
You are the woman who makes up words.
You are the woman who copies
her cupped palm with her fist in clay.

I am the woman who makes up words.
You are the woman who shapes
a drinking bowl with her fist in clay.
I am the woman with rocks in her pockets.

I am the woman who shapes.
I was a baby who knew names.
You are the child with rocks in her pockets.
You are the girl in a plaid dress.

You are the woman who knows names.
You are the baby who could fly.
You are the girl in a plaid dress
upside down on the monkey bars.

You are the baby who could fly
over the moon from a swinging perch
upside down on the monkey bars.
You are the baby who eats meat.

Over the moon from a swinging perch
the feathery goblin calls her sister.
You are the baby who eats meat
the bitch wolf hunts and chews for you.

The feathery goblin calls her sister:
"You are braver than your mother.
The bitch wolf hunts and chews for you.
What are you whining about now?"

You are braver than your mother
and I am not a timid woman:
what are you whining about now?
My palms itch with slick anger,

and I'm not a timid woman.
You are the woman I can't mention;
my palms itch with slick anger.
You are the heiress of scraped knees.

You are the woman I can't mention
to a woman I want to love.
You are the heiress of scraped knees:
scrub them in mountain water.

To a woman, I want to love
women you could turn into
scrub them in mountain water,
stroke their astonishing faces.

Women you could turn into
the scare mask of Bad Mother
stroke their astonishing faces
in the silver-scratched sink mirror.

The scare mask of Bad Mother
crumbles to chunked, pinched clay,
sinks in the silver-scratched mirror.
You are the Little Robber Girl who

crumbles the clay chunks, pinches
her friend, gives her a sharp knife.
You are the Little Robber Girl who
was any witch's youngest daughter.

Our friend gives you a sharp knife,
shows how the useful blades open.
Was any witch's youngest daughter
golden and bold as you? You run and

show how the useful blades open.
You are the baby on the mountain. I am
golden and bold as you. You run and
we pace each other for a long time.

The Hang-Glider's Daughter

for Catherine Logan

My forty-year-old father learned to fly.
Bat-winged, with a magic marble fear
keeping his toast down, he walks off a sheer
shaved cliff into the morning. On Sunday
mornings he comes for us. Liane and I
feed the baby and Mario, wash up, clear
the kitchen mess. Maman is never there;
that is the morning she and Joseph try
to tell the other pickers how the Word
can save them. Liane gets me good and mad
changing her outfit sixteen times, while I
have to change the baby. All the way
up the hill road she practices on him, flirt-
ing like she does at school. My back teeth hurt

from chewing Pepper Gum on the bad side.
She's three years younger. I'm three years behind.
Did he *mean* that? Shift the gum. Did I remind
Mario, if the baby cries, he needs
burping? I can stretch out on the back seat.
The olive terraces stacked in the sunshine
are shallow stairs a giant child could climb.
My hiking shoes look giant on my feet.
Maman says "a missed boy." What do I miss?
I wonder what the word in English is
for that. Funny, that we should have been born
somewhere we wouldn't even understand
the language now. I was already three
when we left. If someone hypnotized me

would I talk English like a three-year-old?
The bright road twists up; bumpily we shift
gears, breathe deep. In the front pouch of my sweat-
shirt, I've still got my two best marbles. Rolled
in thumb and finger, they click, points gained, told
beads. Not for Joseph's church. If I forgot
French, too, who would I be inside my head?
My hands remember better: how to hold
my penknife to strip branches, where to crack
eggs on a bowl rim, how to pile a block
tower—when I was little—high as my nose.
Could I, still? The box of blocks is Mario's
now. My knee's cramped. I wish that I could walk
to Dad's house, or that I was up front, talk-

ing to him. How does he feel, suddenly slung
from brilliant nylon, levering onto air
currents like a thinking hawk? I'd be scared.
I'd be so scared I can't think it. Maybe a long
slope on my skateboard's like that. Climbing
isn't scary: no time. The air's fizzy, you're care-
ful what rock you hang your weight from, and where
your toes wedge. My calves ache, after, ribs sting,
but I'm good for something. What I like high
is mountains. I'll go up the hill behind
Dad's house this afternoon. I'll pick Liane
flowers. Nahh, we'll be leafing magazines
for school clothes on the sunporch after lunch.
I like those purple bell-spikes. My cleats crunch

the crumble; I stretch to the ledge and pull
out the whole rooted stalk. Sometimes there's twelve
bells, purple as—purple as nothing else
except a flower, ugly and beautiful

at once. Across my face come the two smells:
grandmother's linen-chest spice-sweet petals
and wet dirt clinging, half meat, half metal,
all raw. Between them, I smell myself,
sweaty from climbing, but it's a woman's
sweat. I had one of the moon dreams again.
I stood on the flyover facing purple
sea, head up, while a house-huge full moon hurtled
toward me; then it was me flying, feet still
on the road. We're here, on top of the hill.

Lines Declining a Transatlantic
Dinner Invitation

for Charlie and Tom

Regretfully, I proffer my excuses.
Number not less than Graces, more than Muses:
Auden's casting call for a dinner party.
He was a genius who was often smart. He
did not think hosts should count their guests in pairs,
unless they had love seats and no hard chairs.
He was benignly daft for Small Odd Numbers:
a table choked with elbows soon encumbers
wit. I'm sure you'll all be very witty.
I'll miss it, snowed in here in New York City.
But, being *d'un certain age,* we come to know:
better to be discussed than be *de trop.*
The unexpected often is disaster.
If one arrives a month or an hour faster
than looked for, something that one cannot like
might happen: cab drivers would be on strike;
one's friends would be that morning reconciled
with lover, spouse, or adolescent child,
whose tears, A-Levels, or Social Disease
will call them home before the fruit and cheese;
the woman-poet-hating editor
looms ominously near the kitchen door
where a zinc bucket slops up the cold rain
that's sluiced down since the roof fell in again;
one host is wrapped in blankets in the attic: a
damp-inspired episode of his sciatica;
the other, peeling sprouts in a clogged sink,
scowls through a fourth compensatory drink;

somebody else has brought along a new
chum who was scathing in *The New Review;*
there'd be the flight to Amsterdam at nine;
simply, there might be insufficient wine.
As passports take two weeks to put in shape,
this all may have a flavor of sour grape.
Speaking of grapes—I hope you bought *Biscuit*—
pour one more brandy, as it were, on me.

Iva's Birthday Poem

All horns should honk like anything!
All taxicabs should come alive
and stand on their back wheels and sing
that Iva Alyxander's five!

The fish are burbling in the lake,
the bees are buzzing in their hive,
the candles flicker on the cake
that Iva Alyxander's five!

She's put on inches, weight, and speed.
Who knows what wonders may arrive.
I prophesy she'll learn to read,
now Iva Alyxander's five.

Dolphins leap in the swimming pool
to watch her famous cartwheel dive.
Jump! Flip! Swirl! Splash! *Extremely* cool,
now Iva Alyxander's five.

She'll hire a plane—she has a plan—
and teach her mother how to drive.
She can, if anybody can,
now Iva Alyxander's five.

She's smart, she's tough, you've got to hand her
that—so praise in prose and verse
the newly five-year-old Commander
(in Training) of the Whole Universe.

The Acrobats, the Metropoli-
tan Opera and the Royal Ballet
will jointly stage a birthday gala,
for you-know-who is five today!

Wonder Woman and Superman
and Robot Warriors from Mars
all pick up rainbow spray-paint cans
and write her name on subway cars.

They hand out ice cream in the station
with chocolate bars as big as bricks.
There won't be such a celebration
till Iva Alyxander's six!

We'll toast her health! So pour a drink of
Champagne, or chocolate soda! I've
the greatest daughter I can think of
and Iva Alyxander's FIVE!!!!!

Partial Analysis

(of the "Giudizio Universale" of Giovanni di Paolo)

for Richard Howard

Do you imagine, wakeful late in bed,
a Gay Bar Paradiso, inlaid gold,
or are you inexplicably impelled
to Hell, where naked people eat boiled toad?

Beneath six trees in fruit with golden apples,
two boys are stroked by a graybeard schoolmaster.
A Carmelite comes up behind her sister
(praying) and smooths her cowl and cups her nipples.

A monk is taking off another monk's
belt. Two svelte blond maidens, looking rapt,
caress each other's breasts. Pink incorrupt-
ible chubby martyred Innocents give thanks.

A nun, an Arab, and a bearded priest
exchange a blessing that goes round three ways.
Three angels have three monks down on their knees.
A cardinal greets a youth with a slim waist

cinctured in red. In Hell, it's very dark
and pasty-looking people with no clothes
are pinched and pushed and boiled in noxious baths
—it's not unlike some places in New York—

while everyone looks put upon or bored.
But everyone looks Interestingly Bad
in Heaven, their reward for being good:
Hesperidean light, and no holds barred.

Why We Are Going Back
to Paradise Island

He has just cornered and skewered
a rat with a broomstick. He once shot
a milk doe, sloppily and badly.
He let his cousin's kitten starve, to show him.
Stalking at dawn in March, when he was twelve,
he shot his small brother by mistake.

He mourns his son, dead twelve hours old,
his father gulping in an oxygen
tent, the brother whose surprised
gasp explodes his waking lips again.
He hunts them down in dreams. His fat smart
baby daughter wanders in front of a truck

so he buys an identical pickup truck
and picks up another older little daughter
aged, say, eight, and drives her out to the woods
behind the motel, and bashes her when she screams.
Does he, really? He imagines
the wind, the smell of moldy birch leaves

and blown smoke. What if he really hated
his wife, if she were nothing but a cunt
and her cunt were a swamp lined with razor blades?
He has two wives, really. One lives on pills.
He pays her therapist. The other has
her ribs taped where he got her with a two-by-four.

Numinous and glowing, stained-glass windows,
poems crafted and spare as winter birch,

he imagines the rapist, the voyeur,
the child-murderer, the telephonist
whispering threats in the night. He imagines
hiring someone to do it to his wife

while she screams and pisses herself. No, while
she groans with delight. She takes it in her
mouth, glistening black, twice as big as his.
Would a sheep's hole feel the same, or the cold
tight gap of a beached dog shark, last gasps
coming together, before limp flesh?

He was not the enemy. He was the hurt
idealist, poet, he read the books
you did. His manners were better than mine.
You wanted him to praise you and make you real.
I wanted to hear about his childhood.
We wanted him to love us.

Shirland Road

for Yvonne

This is the other story. There are three
women in a room. Fat glasses, tea-
pot not cleared away, we draw up tides
of talk that clear the beaches and subside
to amicable silence; sip, smoke, lean
back into notebooks, newspapers. The green
unfabled garden darkens. One of the cats
thumps in the window, rumbles on a mat-
ted cushion near the red bars of the fire.
Beyond the magic circle of desire
where shadows stall in storied attitudes,
this continues happening. Warmed blood
unclenches toes and fingers, which can stroke
cat, cushion, massed black hair tangled with smoke
and rosewater. You have strewn secondhand
treasures on all your surfaces, that find,
question, dismiss the eye; buff, blue, brown things
I like. Have we been quiet for a long
time? Vermouth, Eleanor of Aquitaine.
A red moth skitters on the windowpane.
Brown flowers glow on globed light above strewn books.
Marie is writing, too. You've gone to cook
supper: brown garlic, slice a cucumber.
I track my nose into the kitchen, stir
up salad dressing, filch a corner of cheese,
teetering on a balance bridging these
planks of resignation and repose.

La Fontaine de Vaucluse

for Marie Ponsot

Why write unless you praise the sacred places . . . ?
Richard Howard, "Audiences"

I

Azure striation swirls beyond the stones
flung in by French papas and German boys.
The radio guide emits trilingual noise.
"Always 'two ladies alone'; we were not alone."
Source, cunt, umbilicus, resilient blue
springs where the sheer gorge spreads wooded, mossed
          thighs:
unsounded female depth in a child-sized
pool boys throw rocks at. Hobbled in platform shoes,
girls stare from the edge. We came for the day
on a hot bus from Avignon. A Swed-
ish child hurls a chalk boulder; a tall girl,
his sister, twelve, tanned, crouches to finger shell
whorls bedded in rock moss. We find our way
here when we can; we take away what we need.

II
Here, when we can, we take away what we need:
stones, jars of herb leaves, scrap-patch workbags stored
in the haphazard rooms we can afford.
Marie and I are lucky: we can feed
our children and ourselves on what we earn.
One left the man who beat her, left hostages
two daughters; one weighs her life to her wages,
finds both wanting and, bought out, stays put, scorn-
ful of herself for not deserving more.
The concierge at Le Régent is forty-six;
there fifteen years, widowed for one, behind
counters a dun perpetual presence, fixed
in sallow non-age till Marie talked to her.
I learn she is coeval with my friends.

III
I learn she is coeval with my friends:
the novelist of seventy who gives
us tea and cakes; the sister with whom she lives
a dialogue; the old Hungarian
countess's potter daughter, British, dyke,
bravely espoused in a medieval hill
town in Provence; Jane whom I probably will
never know and would probably never like;
Liliane the weaver; Liliane's daughter
the weaver; Liliane's housewifely other
daughter, mothering; the great-grandmother
who drove us through gnarled lanes at Avignon;
the virgin at the source with wedgies on;
Iva, who will want to know what I brought her.

IV

Iva, who will want to know what I brought her
(from Selfridge's, a double-decker bus,
a taxi, Lego; a dark-blue flowered dress
from Uniprix; a wickerwork doll's chair
from the Vence market; books; a wrapped-yarn deer;
a batik: girl guitarist who composes
sea creatures, one of three I chose,
two by the pupil, one by the woman who taught her),
might plunge her arms to the elbows, might shy stones,
might stay shy. I'll see her in ten days.
Sometimes she still swims at my center; sometimes
she is a four-year-old an ocean away
and I am on vertiginous terrain
where I am nobody's mother and nobody's daughter.

V

"Where I am, nobody's mother and nobody's daughter
can find me," words of a woman in pain
or self-blame, obsessed with an absent or present man,
blindfolded, crossing two swords, her back to the water.
The truth is, I wake up with lust and loss
and only half believe in something better;
the truth is that I still write twelve-page letters
and blame my acne and my flabby ass
that I am thirty-five and celibate.
Women are lustful and fickle and all alike,
say the hand-laid flower-pressed sheets at the paper mill.
I pay attention to what lies they tell
us here, but at the flowered lip, hesitate,
one of the tamed girls stopped at the edge to look.

VI

One of the tamed girls stopped at the edge to look
at her self in the water, genital self that stains
and stinks, that is synonymous with drains,
wounds, pettiness, stupidity, rebuke.
The pool creates itself, cleansed, puissant, deep
as magma, maker, genetrix. Marie
and I, each with a notebook on her knee,
begin to write, homage the source calls up
or force we find here. There is another source
consecrate in the pool we perch above:
our own intelligent accord that brings
us to the lucid power of the spring
to work at reinventing work and love.
We may be learning how to tell the truth.

VII

We may be learning how to tell the truth.
Distracted by a cinematic sky,
Paris below two dozen shades of gray,
in borrowed rooms we couldn't afford, we both
work over words till we can tell ourselves
what we saw. I get up at eight, go down
to buy fresh croissants, put a saucepan on
and brew first shared coffee. The water solves
itself, salves us. Sideways, hugging the bank,
two stocky women helped each other, drank
from leathery cupped palms. We make our own
descent downstream, getting our shoes wet, care-
fully hoist cold handsful from a crevice where
azure striation swirls beyond the stones.

Peterborough

Another story still: a porch with trees
—maple and oak, sharpening younger shoots
against the screen; privileged solitude
with early sunlight pouring in a thin
wash on flat leaves like milk on a child's chin.
Light shifts and dulls. I want to love a woman
with my radical skin, reactionary im-
agination. My body is cored with hunger;
my mind is gnarled in oily knots of anger
that push back words: inelegant defeat
of female aspiration. First we're taught
men's love is what we cannot do without;
obliged to do without precisely that:
too fat, too smart, too loud, too shy, too old.
Unloved and underpaid, tonight untold
women will click our failings off, each bead
inflating to a bathysphere, our need
encapsulated in a metal skin,
which we, subaqueous monsters, cannot in-
filtrate. The middle of the road is noon.
Reactive creature with inconstant moon
tides (no doubt amendable as near-
sightedness, but sacred to How Things Are)
my blood came down and I swarmed up a tree,
intoxicated with maturity.
Woman? Well, maybe—but I was a Grown-
Up, entitled to make up my own
mind, manners, morals, myths—menses small price
to pay for midnight and my own advice.
By next September, something was revenged

on me. Muffled in sweat-soaked wool, I lunged
out of seventh-grade science lab, just quick
enough to get to the Girls' Room and be sick.
Blotched cheeks sucked to my teeth, intestines turn-
ing themselves out, hunched over a churn-
ing womb fisting itself, not quite thirteen,
my green age turned me regularly green.
Our Jewish man G.P. to whom I carried
myself hinted sex helped, once you were married.
Those weren't days I fancied getting laid.
Feet pillowed up, belly on heating pad,
head lolled toward Russian novel on the floor,
I served my time each hour of the four
days of the week of the month for the next ten
years, during which I fucked a dozen men,
not therapeutically, and just as well.
Married to boot, each month still hurt like hell.
The sky thickens, seeps rain. I retrospective-
ly add my annals to our tribe's collective
Book of Passage Rites, and do not say
a woman gave notebook leaves to me today
whose argument was what I knew: desire,
and all the old excuses ranked, conspired:
avoid, misunderstand, procrastinate;
say you're monogamous, or celibate,
sex is too messy, better to be friends
(thirsty for drafts of amity beyond
this hesitation, which has less to do
with her than my quixotic body's too
pertinacious—*tua tam pertinax
valetudo*, neither forward nor back-
ward—malingering, I ask, or healing).
I like her: smart, strong, sane, companionate.
I still love a man: true, but irrelevant.

Then, unavoidably, why not?
She was gone (of course) by this time; I sat
mirrored, eye-to-eye, cornered between
two scalp-high windows framing persistent rain.

Home, and I've

Covered the flowered linen
where I graze
on a convolvulus that hides in
lion grass, and ride in-

to the sunrise on a sand
horse. These days
shorten, but the afternoon simmered
me down. I had dinner

alone, with retrospective
on the blaz-
on of your throat's tiger-lily flush
and your salt sap enough

company until tomorrow.
The fat blue
lamp spills on a ziggurat of books,
mug the same cobalt. Looks

like reprise of lesson one
in how to
keep on keeping on. Easier, with
you fixed hours away; both

solitude and company
have a new
savor: yours. Sweet woman, I'll woman-
fully word a nomen-

clature for what we're doing
when we come
to; come to each other with our eyes,
ears, arms, minds, everything wide

open. Your tonic augments
my humdrum
incantations till they work. I can
stop envying the man

whose berth's the lap where I'd like
to roll home
tonight. I've got May's new book for bed,
steak, greens, and wine inside

me, you back tomorrow, some
words,some laz-
y time (prune the plants, hear Mozart) to
indulge in missing you.

Pantoum

There is a serviceable wooden dory
rocking gently at the lip of ocean,
from where her moor line loops back loosely
to an outrider of the wet forest.

Rocking gently at the lip of ocean,
whorled and rosy carapaces glimmer.
To an outrider of the wet forest
who kneels at the undulant flat belly

whorled and rosy carapaces glimmer
under, the water is a mirror dreaming.
Who kneels at the undulant flat belly
feels her pulse gyre in the liquid circles.

Under the water is a mirror dreaming
furled leaves. She kneads and presses her friend's spine,
feels her pulse gyre in the liquid circles
her palm oils on smooth skin, opening like

furled leaves. She kneads and presses her friend's spine,
enters her own blood's tiderush, leaves
her palm oils on smooth skin. Opening like
shrubbery parting to bare fingers, she

enters. Her own blood's tiderush leaves
her charged with flammable air, igniting the
shrubbery. Parting to bare fingers, she
grows, reaches into the fire licking

her, charged with flammable air, igniting the
dry tinder, and the wet places that flame like brandy.
Grows, reaches into the fire licking
her clean, that nourishes as it consumes

dry tinder. And the wet places that flame like brandy
are knowledgeable. They affirm
her: clean. That nourishes as it consumes
detritus of self-doubt, whispers she fears

are knowledgeable. They affirm
each other in themselves. Still, when the
detritus of self-doubt whispers, she fears
the empty pool, that secret. They could lose

each other in themselves, still. When the
postcards begin arriving, they depict
the empty pool, that secret. They could lose
jobs, balance, money, central words, music.

Postcards begin arriving. They depict
themselves living in a perfect landscape, with
jobs, balance, money: central. Words, music
one made for the other, late at night, as they rocked

themselves. Living in a perfect landscape, with
passionate friends, you'd ache, she thinks.
One made for the other? Late at night, as they rocked
into incognate languages, were they still

passionate friends? You'd ache, she thinks,
if your mind buzzed with translations of denial
into incognate languages. Were they still
anywhere near the hidden rainforest?

If your mind buzzed with translations of denial,
you might not see the gapping in the hedgerows,
anywhere near the hidden rainforest,
a child could push through, or a tall woman stooping.

You might not see the gapping in the hedgerows
at first. She grew up here, points out where
a child could push through, or a tall woman. Stooping,
howevermany shoulder in, to the brambles

at first. She grew up here, points out where
the path mounts, damp under eye-high ferns.
However many shoulder into the brambles,
each one inhales the solitude of climbing.

The path mounts, damp under eye-high ferns.
Cedars aspire to vanishing point in the sky.
Each one inhales the solitude of climbing
lichenous rocks. In soft perpetual rain,

cedars aspire to vanishing point in the sky,
then, sea-stained and enormous, niched for foothold,
lichenous rocks, in soft perpetual rain.
Each, agile or clumsy, silently scales them.

Then, see: stained and enormous, niched for foothold
by tide pools sloshing broken shells and driftwood
(each, agile or clumsy, silently scales them
to her own size), boulders embrace the sound.

By tide pools sloshing broken shells, and driftwood
from where her moor line loops back loosely
to her own sides (boulders embrace the sound
there) is a serviceable wooden dory.

Canzone

Consider the three functions of the tongue:
taste, speech, the telegraphy of pleasure,
are not confused in any human tongue;
yet, sinewy and singular, the tongue
accomplishes what, perhaps, no other organ
can. Were I to speak of giving tongue,
you'd think two things at least; and a cooked tongue,
sliced, on a plate, with caper sauce, which I give
my guest for lunch, is one more, to which she'd give
the careful concentration of her tongue
twice over, to appreciate the taste
and to express—it would be in good taste—

a gastronomic memory the taste
called to mind, and mind brought back to tongue.
There is a paucity of words for taste:
sweet, sour, bitter, salty. Any taste,
however multiplicitous its pleasure,
complex its execution (I might taste
that sauce ten times in cooking, change its taste
with herbal subtleties, chromatic organ
tones of clove and basil, good with organ
meats) must be described with those few taste
words, or with metaphors, to give
my version of sensations it would give

a neophyte, deciding whether to give
it a try. She might develop a taste.
(You try things once; I think you have to give
two chances, though, to know your mind, or give

up on novelties.) Your mother tongue
nurtures, has the subtleties which give
flavor to words, and words to flavor, give
the by no means subsidiary pleasure
of being able to describe a pleasure
and re-create it. Making words, we give
the private contemplations of each organ
to the others, and to others, organ-

ize sensations into thoughts. Sentient organ-
isms, we symbolize feeling, give
the spectrum (that's a symbol) each sense organ
perceives, by analogy, to others. Disorgan-
ization of the senses is an acquired taste
we all acquire: as speaking beasts, it's organ-
ic to our discourse. The first organ
of acknowledged communion is the tongue
(tripartite diplomat, which after tongu-
ing a less voluble expressive organ
to wordless efflorescences of pleasure
offers up words to reaffirm the pleasure).

That's a primary difficulty: pleasure
means something, and something different, for each organ;
each person, too. I may take exquisite pleasure
in boiled eel, or blancmange—or not. One pleasure
of language is making known what not to give.
And think of a bar of lavender soap, a pleasure
to see and, moistened, rub on your skin, a pleasure
especially to smell, but if you taste
it (though smell is most akin to taste)
what you experience will not be pleasure;
you almost retch, grimace, stick out your tongue,
slosh rinses of ice water over your tongue.

But I would rather think about your tongue
experiencing and transmitting pleasure
to one or another multisensual organ
—like memory. Whoever wants to give
only one meaning to that has untutored taste.

from Taking Notice

two women together is a work
nothing in civilization has made simple

Adrienne Rich, *XXI Love Poems*

I

My child wants dolls, a tutu, that girls' world made
pretty and facile. Sometimes. Sometimes I
want you around uncomplicatedly.
Work every day; love (the same one) every
night: old songs and new choir the parade
of coupled women whose fidelity
is a dyke icon. You are right: if we
came to new love and friendship with a sad
baggage of endings, we would come in bad
faith, and bring, rooted already, seed
of a splitting. Serial monogamy
is a cogwheeled hurt, though you don't like the word.
The neighbor's tireless radio sings lies
through the thin wall behind my desk and bed.

II

Morning: the phone jangles me from words: you,
working at his place, where you slept last night,
missed me. You'll bring drawings. I missed you too.
What centers, palpably swelling my tight
chest: lust, tenderness, an itch of tears.
Three Swedish ivy rootlings get a pot.
Wash earth-crumbed hands, strip, put long underwear
on, tug, zip, buckle, tie, button, go out—
a mailbox full of bills and circulars.
I trust you: it's a knife edge of surprise
through words I couldn't write down, subvocalize
across Eighty-First Street, cold as it was
at eight when I put Iva on the bus,
stalling through iced slush between frost-rimed cars.

III

When that jackbooted choreography
sends hobnailed cabrioles across a brain,
the stroked iron pulling lovers together pulls
them apart. Through the ecstatic reverie
of hands, eyes, mouths, our surfaces' silken
sparking, heraldic plants and animals
alive on our tender cartography,
the homesick victim glimpses the coast of pain,
hears the familiar argot of denial.
Woman I love, as old, as new to me
as any moment of delight risked in
my lumpy heretofore unbeautiful
skin, if I lost myself in you I'd be
no better lost than any other woman.

IV

She twists scraps of her hair in unshelled snails
crossed by two hairpins. It takes forty-five
minutes. I'm twelve. I've come in to pee. I've
left *Amazing Stories* and *Weird Tales*
in the hamper. "Don't believe what you read.
Women who let men use them are worse than
whores. Men despise them. I can understand
prostitutes, never 'free love.' " Not freed
to tell her what I thought of *More Than Human*,
I wipe between my mottled oversized
girl haunches. I'll be one of the despised,
I know, as she forbids with her woman's
body, flaccid, gaunt in a grayed nightgown,
something more culpable for us than "men."

V

"I never will be only a Lesbian."
Bare rubber, wedged beside its tube of cream
in the bookshelf near your bed, your diaphragm
lies on Jane Cooper's poem and Gertrude Stein.
I've torn our warm cocoon again. I listen.
Our sweatered breasts nuzzle under the quilt.
(Yes, there's one in my bathroom cabinet;
unused, now.) If a man sleeps with men, and women,
he's *queer: vide* Wilde, Goodman, Gide, Verlaine.
A woman who does can be "passionately
heterosexual" (said Norman Pearson of H. D.).
Anyone's love with women doesn't count.
Rhetoric, this. You talk about your friend.
I hold you, wanting whatever I want.

VI

Angry, I speak, and pass the hurt to you,
your pencil-smudged face naked like a child's.
Each time we don't know what we're getting into
or out of. Later, washed out and reconciled,
we wait on the subway platform, Mutt and Jeff
puffed out with football socks and Duofolds,
word-shy, habitually bold enough
to sit thigh against corduroy thigh and hold
hands; though, ungendered in thick winter gear,
only your cheeks' epicene ivory
makes us the same sex. No one looks healthy
in the perpetual fluorescence. Here
(you say) the light is the same night and day,
but it feels like night at night anyway.

VII

If we talk, we're too tired to make love; if we
make love, these days, there's hardly time to talk.
We sit to share supper once, twice a week.
You're red and white with cold; we're brusque, scared, shy.
Difficult speech curdles the café au lait
next morning. In the short twelve hours between
we rubbed, laughed, tongued, exhorted, listened, came,
slept like packed spoons. Wrapped up against the day
we trudge through slush as far as the downtown
subway, brush cold-tattered lips. You're gone
to hunch sock-shod over your camera while
I stare a spiral notebook down six miles
north, indulging some rich weave of weeks where
we'd work, play, not cross-reference calendars.

X

The grizzled doorman lets the doctors' wives
into and out of the rainstorm. Thirty-year-
old mothers hive here till their men's careers
regroup the swarm for boxed suburban lives.
The doorman's sixty, football-shouldered, white.
The multiracial anoraked interns
will earn, per year, at forty, more than he earns
in ten. Maybe one-tenth of the scrubbed bright
wives will earn his wages; fewer do.
Knees dovetailed at The Duchess, I'm giving you
my hours with a talk-starved woman I knew there
through her tough small girl, while on the polished square
at our boot-toes blue-jeaned women slow-dance
to a rhythmic alto plaint of ruined romance.

XIII

No better lost than any other woman
turned resolutely from the common pool
of our erased, emended history,
I think of water, in this book-strewn room. In
another room, my daughter, home from school,
audibly murmurs "spanking, stupid, angry
voice"—a closet drama where I am
played secondhand to unresisting doll
daughters. Mother and daughter both, I see
myself, the furious and unforgiven;
myself, the terrified and terrible;
the child punished into autonomy;
the unhealed woman hearing her own voice damn
her to the nightmares of the brooding girl.

XIV

And I shout at Iva, whine at you. Easily
we choose up for nuclear family,
with me the indirect, sniveling, put-upon
mother/wife, child's villain, feminist heroine,
bore. On thick white plates the failed communion
congeals. Iva bawls in her room. You're on
edge, worked out, fed up, could leave. Shakily
we stop. You wash dishes, drop one; it breaks. We
should laugh. We don't. A potted plant crashed too.
Frowning, I salvage the crushed shoots while you
deflect my scowl with yours. You leave a phone
message for your friend while I read one
last picture book, permit a bedtime drink
to a nude child, who's forgiven me—I think.

XVIII

I'll tell you what I don't want: an affair:
love, by appointment only, twice a week;
grimy, gratuitous life lived elsewhere
with others. When it's easier to speak
about than to you, when I think of you
more than I'm with you, more anxious than tender,
I feel less than a friend. There's work to do.
Artist, woman, I love you; craft and gender,
if we're antagonists, aren't in dispute.
Love starts with circumstance; it grows with care
to something self-sufficient, centered, root
from which the cultivators branch, the air
renewing them transpired rich from its pores.
Or so I hoped while I was celibate.

XIX

When I read poems to the art students
I wanted you there; when my ephebes, shar-
ing craft I taught, showed off, I wanted you there;
when I talk a woman around imprudence,
when I orchestrate a meeting or a meal,
when my thoughts unroll imaginal sentences,
when I come through better than I thought I was,
I want you there. But I surface seasick, feel
desire and apprehension lashed like stones
to me. Reeled toward you in the elevator,
I shrink inches from my accomplished stature
of thoughtful hero, whom you haven't seen,
diminishing to needy lover, green
with doubt and necessarily alone.

XXIII

As yoked to her by absence as by presence,
I image, fifteen minutes since she's gone,
her sneakers pushing leaves up as she ran
into the woods, urged on to independence
by me. Feet on the porch rail, I drink silence,
thinking: She has to cross the road alone.
If she doesn't find anyone at home
—the six-year-old gone shopping with his parents—
will she get panicky and lose her way?
Revenant, you nap. Marie drove to town.
I look up from my book, identify
the she-cardinal's sanguine rose brown,
then check my watch. From down the path comes "Hey,
Mom!" Forty-five minutes on my own.

F R O M

ASSUMPTIONS

1 9 8 5

Towards Autumn

Mid-September, and I miss my daughter.
I sit out on the terrace with my friend,
talking, with morning tea, coffee, and bread,
about another woman, and her mother,
who survived heroism; her lover
who will have to. I surprise myself

with language; lacking it, don't like myself
much. I owe a letter to my daughter.
Thinking of her's like thinking of a lover
I hope will someday grow to be a friend.
I missed the words to make friends with my mother.
I pull the long knife through the mound of bread,

spoon my slice with cherry preserves, the bread
chewy as meat beneath, remind myself
I've errands for our ancient patron, mother
of dramas, hard mother to a daughter
twenty years my senior, who is my friend,
who lives in exile with a woman lover

also my friend, three miles from here. A lover
of good bread, my (present) friend leaves this bread
and marmalades *biscottes*. To have a friend
a generation older than myself
is sometimes like a letter for my daughter
to read, when she can read: What your mother

left undone, women who are not your mother
may do. Women who are not your lover

love you. (That's to myself, and my daughter.)
We take coffee- and teapot, mugs, jam jars, bread
inside, wash up. I've work, hours by myself.
Beyond the kitchen, in her room, my friend

writes, overlooking the same hills. Befriend
yourself: I couldn't have known to tell my mother
that, unless I'd learned it for myself.
Until I do. Friendship is earned. A lover
leaps into faith. Earthbound women share bread;
make; do. Cherry compote would please my daughter.

My daughter was born hero to her mother;
found, like a lover, flawed; found, like a friend,
faithful as bread I'd learn to make myself.

Fourteen

We shopped for dresses which were always wrong:
sweatshop approximations of the lean-
lined girls' wear I studied in *Seventeen*.
The armholes pinched, the belt didn't belong,
the skirt drooped forward (I'd be told at school).
Our odd-lot bargains deformed the image,
but she and I loved Saturday rummage.
One day she listed outside Loehmann's. Drool
wet her chin. Stumbling, she screamed at me. Dropping
our parcels on the pavement, she fell in
what looked like a fit. I guessed: insulin.
The cop said, "Drunk," and called an ambulance
while she cursed me and slapped away my hands.
When I need a mother, I still go shopping.

Mother

I was born when she was thirty-eight.
Pleated secrets sunlit on a skirt
spread over rocks, dark curls, sharp nose, alert
shopgirl's cautious mouth curve. She had to wait
between high school and college, married late
—thirty-one—motherless teenaged, serving
father, time black-frocked at Macy's, deserving
Jewish daughter. Patience: her great
longings encysted with it, burst. I'll be
thirty-eight in November. In her head
whir words she learned, memorized, accented
impeccably out of the Bronx. In the Bronx she
rages, shrunken, pillow-propped, in a rank
room. I invent freedom at the bank.

I invent stories she will never tell.
I was fatherless; she was motherless.
I thought that I was motherless as well.
Harridan, pin-curled in a washed-out housedress,
she scrubbed the tiny kitchen on all fours
and sniped. I bolted. I told dog walkers,
as I chipped bark flakes from the sycamore
out front, such stories! I do not know hers.
The mother says, "When I was twenty, I . . ."
The daughter, "I was . . . I never thought you . . ."
"My best friend . . ." "I was afraid. Tell me why . . . ?"
". . . I was afraid." Twined down the long wind go
fictions, afternoon lies the nurse tells to
a furious old woman, who will die.

Days of 1959

He had devirginated my friend Nan.
Nuyorican, gorgeous, all parts made small,
he was married to a round-shouldered, tall-
er-than-he-was WASP science-fiction fan,
a saccharine-frosted Lauren Bacall
who filed while "Le Théâtre du Vingtième
Siècle" caused my proximity to him.
I knew enough to be a know-it-all
maiden adulteress with diaphragm
in their East Third Street bed before midterm.
"Starbright, I hope I have someone like you
to love me when I'm fifty." He didn't mean
me; he meant, some girl under eighteen.
Somewhere or other, he is fifty now.

He's fifty somewhere now; perhaps he has;
unless the dope that he commenced to do
at twenty-five did him. Sartre and jazz
played into idiot opiates, right out
of that South Bronx he never talked about.
He left his wife, but she was shooting too,
by then. Once his initiate in grass,
I was a has-been hanger-on, ignored
uptown in all-night diners while he scored,
then "A" down, West Bronx "D" back home, lone Jew-
ess on the milk train; south to class
next day, badly prepared except to doubt
practically anything anyone knew.
I snorted once; was, by some blessing, bored.

Fifteen to Eighteen

I'd almost know, the nights I snuck in late,
at two, at three, as soon as I had tucked
into myself tucked in, to masturbate
and make happen what hadn't when I fucked,
there'd be the gargled cry, always "God damn
you to hell," to start with, from the other
bedroom: she was in shock again. I swam
to my surface to take care of my mother.
That meant, run for a glass of orange juice,
clamp her shoulders with one arm, try to pour
it down her throat while she screamed "No, God damn
you!" She is stronger than I am
when this happens. If she rolls off on the floor,
I can't / she won't let me / lift her up. Fructose
solution, a shot and she'd come around.
At half past two, what doctor could I call?
Sometimes I had to call the hospital.
More often, enough orange juice got down,
splashed on us both.
                              "What are you doing here?
Where were you? Why is my bed in this mess?
How did you get those scratches on your face?
What were you doing, out until this hour?"

1973

"I'm pregnant," I wrote to her in delight
from London, thirty, married, in print. A fools-
cap sheet scrawled slantwise with one minuscule
sentence came back. "I hope your child is white."
I couldn't tear the pieces small enough.
I hoped she'd be black as the ace of spades,
though hybrid beige heredity had made
that as unlikely as the spun-gold stuff
sprouted after her neonatal fur.
I grudgingly acknowledged her "good hair,"
which wasn't, very, from my point of view.
"No tar brush left," her father's mother said.
"She's Jewish and she's white," from her cranked bed
mine smugly snapped.
　　　　　　　　　　　She's Black. She is a Jew.

Mother II

No one is "Woman" to another
woman, except her mother.
Her breasts were unmysterious
naked: limp, small. But I thought pus
must ooze from them: her underwear
like bandages. Blood came from where
I came from, stanched with pads between
her legs, under the girdle, seen
through gaping bathroom doors. Around
her waist, all sorts of rubber. Bound
to stop the milk, my milk, her breasts
stayed flat. I watched my round self, guessed
a future where I'd droop and leak.
But dry and cool against her cheek
I'd lean my cheek. I stroked the lace
and serge she sheathed her carapace
with: straight skirts, close cuffs, full sleeves;
was, wordless, catechized; believed:
nude, she was gaunt; dressed, she was slim;
nude, she was flabby; dressed, her firm
body matched her brisk, precise
midcontinental teacher's voice,
which she had molded, dry, perfect-
ed from a swamp of dialect.
Naked or clad, for me, she wore
her gender, perpetual chador,
her individual complex
history curtained off by sex.
Child, I determined that I would
not be subsumed in womanhood.

Whatever she was, I was not.
Whoever she was, I forgot
to ask, and she forgot to tell,
muffled in costumes she as well
rejected as a girl, resumed
—on my account? Are women doomed,
beasts that repeat ourselves, to rage
in youth against our own old age,
in age to circumscribe our youth
with self-despisal dressed as truth?
Am I "Woman" to my water-
dwelling brown loquacious daughter,
corporeal exemplar of
her thirst for what she would not love?

Autumn 1980

for Judith McDaniel

I spent the night after my mother died
in a farmhouse north of Saratoga Springs
belonging to a thirty-nine-year-old
professor with long, silvered wiry hair,
a lively girl's flushed cheeks and gemstone eyes.
I didn't know that she had died.
Two big bitches and a varying
heap of cats snoozed near a black woodstove
on a rag rug, while, on the spring-shot couch,
we talked late over slow glasses of wine.
In the spare room near Saratoga Springs
was a high box bed. My mother died
that morning, of heart failure, finally.
Insulin shocks burned out her memory.
On the bed, a blue early-century
Texas Star, in a room white and blue
as my flannel pajamas. I'd have worn
the same, but smaller, ten years old at home.
Home was the Bronx, on Eastburn Avenue,
miles south of the hermetic not-quite-new
block where they'd sent this morning's ambulance.
Her nurse had telephoned. My coat was on,
my book-stuffed bag already on my back.
She said, "Your mother had another shock.
We'll be taking her to the hospital."
I asked if I should stay. She said, "It's all
right." I named the upstate college where
I'd speak that night. This had happened before.
I knew / I didn't know: it's not the same.

November cold was in that corner room
upstairs, with a frame window over land
the woman and another woman owned
—who was away. I thought of her alone
in her wide old bed, me in mine. I turned
the covers back. I didn't know she had died.
The tan dog chased cats; she had to be tied
in the front yard while I went along
on morning errands until, back in town,
I'd catch my bus. November hills were raw
fall after celebratory fall
foliage, reunions, festival.
I blew warmth on my hands in a dark barn
where two shaggy mares whuffled in straw,
dipped steaming velvet muzzles to the pail
of feed. We'd left the pickup's heater on.
It smelled like kapok when we climbed inside.
We both unzipped our parkas for the ride
back to the Saratoga bus station.
I blamed the wind if I felt something wrong.
A shrunken-souled old woman whom I saw
once a month lay on a hospital
slab in the Bronx. Mean or not, that soul
in its cortege of history was gone.
I didn't know that I could never know,
now, the daughtering magic to recall
across two coffee mugs the clever Young
Socialist whose views would coincide
with mine. I didn't know that she had died.
Not talking much, while weighted sky pressed down,
we climbed the back road's bosom to the all-
night diner doubling as a bus depot.
I brushed my new friend's cool cheek with my own,
and caught the southbound bus from Montreal.

I counted boarded-up racetrack motel
after motel. I couldn't read. I tried
to sleep. I didn't know that she had died.
Hours later, outside Port Authority,
rained on, I zipped and hooded an obscure
ache from my right temple down my shoulder.
Anonymous in the midafternoon
crowds, I'd walk, to stretch, I thought, downtown.
I rode on the female wave, typically
into Macy's (where forty-five years
past, qualified by her new M.A.
in Chemistry, she'd sold Fine Lingerie),
to browse in Fall Sale bargains for my child,
aged six, size eight, hung brilliantly or piled
like autumn foliage I'd missed somehow,
and knew what I officially didn't know
and put the bright thing down, scalded with tears.

Part of a True Story

for Margaret Delany

We dress UP!

Ntozake Shange

My dear Mrs. Bloomer:
                                        The exigencies
of my life demand rational costume.
I noticed recently upon perusal
of a number of your interesting
journal, *The Lily*, that your radical
bifurcate garment for gentlewomen
is beyond suggestion; not to mince words,
for sale.
            My people, Mrs. Bloomer, are
as well, south of the District, and until
the last and least of us no longer is
chattel, this woman must be radical
to be rational. A woman of color
is gentle as yourself, until provoked.
I have been, since the age of six.
                                        When I,
aged twenty-some, returned to the scene
of my truncated childhood, with the goal
—which I achieved—of bringing forth my mother
and my father from bondage, as I had
my brothers, many of my sisters and
brothers, I was obliged, for my safety
and theirs, to come to them in male attire.
(Does *attire* have gender?) I cannot pass
as other than I am in one respect;
nor would I wish to. It was curious

passing that other way, where I had passed
before: "This gal can haul as heavy a
load as three men or a mule," et cetera.
A Black man is only marginally
more anonymous on a southern road
than a Black woman. Dare I confess, I
liked that marginal anonymity?
Crop-headed in a neutral suit of clothes,
I sat, a stranger at my mother's table,
bearing good news she could not bear to hear
who bore me, till I bared myself as well,
scarred as I was, to loving scrutiny.
Later, I also bore the scrutiny
of the spouse whom I had reluctantly
left; who, free, had forbidden me to go
to freedom. Newly wived, he did not know
me at all, either as woman or as
myself. It's a peculiar thing: to pass
easily, anonymously, from one
life, or mode of life, to another: done
with a forked suit? Night, starvation, a gun
to scare stragglers to courage, sleep in snow
or straw or not at all are what I know
as passage rites. I do what I can,
but I do not wish to be thought a man
again.
       Tonight, four hundred human souls,
still embodied, disembondaged, lie wakeful
or sleep in this rough but hospitable
hospice, this time, taken across water
to free land. You know the name I am called.
The straits do not. We cross them nonetheless.
I have another name now: General;
a task I had first as a nursling: Nurse.

We intend to bring out four hundred more.
I wish to be there. It is efficacious
that I be there. I must be recognized
though: Black, female, and old, or nearly old.
Still, I am of scant use immobilized.
I wish to be relieved of the woolen gown
whose waterlogged skirts and underskirts hold
me so, as well as the Confederate
Army would wish. I was nearly drowned.
Thus, Mrs. Bloomer, my request. Disguise
is not wished, or called for. Compromise,
though unaccustomed, is appropriate
on this occasion. So is the connection
of our aims. I entertain reflection
that, free and Black, I am still disfranchised,
female; a condition I first realized
espoused: bondwoman and freedman, we
embodied it. I transcend limitation.
I am a Black woman, whose education
was late and little: necessity
of adulthood vowed to emancipation
of my people; the larger limitation
imposed by childhood spent in servitude,
leave me comparatively unlettered.
You will receive this missive, dictated
by me to my adjutant, from her
hand, to which I pray you will deliver
the costume I desire.
                         Awaiting your
kind reply, I remain,
                         Yours faithfully,
Harriet Tubman   United States Army
Medical Division   Port Royal Island

Port Royal Island was captured from the Confederacy by the Union Army in 1861 and became a haven for escaped slaves. Harriet Tubman, then aged about forty-one, and the most successful—and hunted—conductor on the Underground Railroad, was sent there by the governor of Massachusetts in 1862. She served as an Army scout and as a nurse and herbal healer in the field hospital established for the freed slaves and wounded soldiers. In 1863, she led a detachment of the Second South Carolina Volunteers, a company composed of Black soldiers under the command of Colonel James Montgomery, in a raid up the Combahee River, with the objectives of destroying the torpedoes with which the Confederate Army had mined the river, and of liberating as many slaves from the coastal farms as could be transported to Port Royal on the gunboats. More than eight hundred were freed. Harriet Tubman thus added the sobriquet "General" to the name of Moses, by which even her commanding officer addressed her.

Shortly afterward, Tubman, who had never learned to read and write, dictated a letter to Boston, ordering a Bloomer suit, because long skirts were a handicap on such a campaign.

Amelia Bloomer, feminist, abolitionist, and originator of the costume which bore her name, was also editor of *The Lily*, a periodical advocating women's rights.

I'd like to express my gratitude to Ann Petry for her biography of Harriet Tubman; its concise information fueled my imagination.

A Chaplet for Judith Landry

Dear Judith:　In sincerest gratitude,
here is the bread-and-butter gift requested.
I wouldn't want our friendship to be tested
because I didn't sit down and get at it. "Rude
and slovenly, with a bad attitude,"
you'd say; although there might be worse things listed
against me if my offering consisted
of cliché justified by platitude.
I'm writing to you from an estuarial
island, where deer graze, pigs rampage, loons sing; land
marsh-bottomed, oyster-bedded, territorial
range of wild horses, freed pets' progeny.
But still I close my eyes and think of England:
where else could we dig into Kedgeree?

Where else could we dig into Kedgeree
with a prolific writer who'd just been
presented, after sherry, to the Queen?
(Next time they meet, she'll be a C.B.E.)
Two raw colonials, my girl and me
quivered respectfully, thrilled to the bone.
That's why we put on everything we owned,
although it was a sultry fifty-three
indoors. To sit by the electric fire,
stroking enchanting Rock-cake, gone quite flat
(sign of advanced achievement in a cat),
and sip Frascati—I could not desire
more! While our natterings didn't dislodge
from the kittens! the kittens! enraptured Squodge.

From the kittens! the kittens! enraptured Squodge
could only be occasionally pried.
(Say, if a Hamley's van pulled up outside,
sent by the Queen, *pour rendre ses hommages*.)
I'm sorry if we left a grubby hodge-
podge of Lego, socks and tracts beside
your easy chair. We're sloppy, but we tried
to be acceptably contained and *sages*.
I liked the Oriental rugs beneath
and upon the table where we ate,
watching daffodils bloom in the teeth
of London bluster beyond French windows.
You liked loud Iva who resists repose.
I liked tall Lurky who stays up too late.

I liked tall Lurky who stays up too late,
although I missed the threatened saxophone
rehearsal. Living, equals, with your grown
daughter, you enlighten me and my eight-
year-old, who've witnessed pairs wasting with hate-
ful wrangling, while we hug and spar our own
infatuation. You were kind to loan
me your featherbed. Under its weight,
I slept like a plowman with my socks on.
Mornings we drank hot coffee-milk from bowls.
The Saturday it rained, we vetoed Kew
and herded Iva, via the Number 2
to look, with Bonnard (recognition shocks) on
interiors domestic as our souls.

Interiors domestic as our souls,
salvaged like postcards of congenial places:
frayed armchairs framing animated faces,
the two-bar fire with fake electric coals.
The kamikaze boys' club that controls
just the survival of the human race is
excluded temporarily. What grace is
implicit in our customary roles
—confidante, chatelaine, cook, hostess, mother—
when, our own women, we have latitude
to choose them and enact them for each other.
Our homes very infrequently are castles.
Having shared yours, we'll pledge ourselves your vassals,
dear Judith, in sincerest gratitude.

Sword

for Toi Derricotte

This golden vengeance is one of those red
niggers like her grandfather who said
of me, "Her people are just off the boat."
He might have said, just off the cattle cars.
Here she is three, bangs her construction boot
against the van she's perched on. He is in lace,
held by a darker nurse, sixty-six years
earlier. Their twice-bright blade of face
astonishes, doubled, between imp ears
the same red-gold (his lock's glassed) curls around.
When she was born he was long darkened; dead
before he tried her honed red-gold, hybrid
of six million dead off the cattle cars,
just off the slave boats, fifteen million drowned.

Inheritances

Iva asks me for stories of her father's
family. I learned them secondhand
—not even a Christian, and not Black.
I think of a reflective membrane: classes,
mirrored, meld. She starts with slavery.
The eight-year-old hunkered in the old man's

barrel staves to hide when the blue horseman
(she breathed in horse) leaned toward her grandfather
to shout, "Old man, you're free!" While slavery
had slipped, a wristlet from the writing hand
of the bisque-beige girl enrolled in Classes
for Young Ladies, in Paris, where her Black

mother was not. Ledgers were in the black;
the permeated membrane not the man,
else childless, who exercised three classes'
prerogatives (landed, white, male) to father
twice the child who, by his power in hand,
was bred to, and released from, slavery.

Iva asks, "Were your parents *for* slavery?
Were *they* slaves? I know they weren't Black."
She puts her suntanned hand against my hand,
compares. "Does 'manumit' mean, just a man
could make slaves free?" I tell her, my father
spoke German in his West Bronx first-grade classes;

my mother worked at Macy's, took night classes
at Hunter, read about Wage Slavery

and Profits in the kitchen, where her father
waited for her to make his breakfast. Black
dresses were required for work. A man
—Jewish, of course—would take her life in hand.

I don't wear any rings on my left hand.
Two copies of notes home from Iva's classes
are sent. Her father lives with a white man,
writes science-fiction novels: slavery
on far worlds, often, though the slaves aren't Black.
She says, "Dad's roommate," or "My other father."

I wouldn't say to a Black friend that class is
(in its erasures) slavery. I hand
down little to emancipate my father.

Graffiti from the Gare Saint-Manqué

for Zed Bee

Outside the vineyard is a caravan
of Germans taking pictures in the rain.
The local cheese is Brillat-Savarin.
The local wine is Savigny-les-Beaune.
We learn Burgundies while we have the chance
and lie down under cabbage-rose wallpaper.
It's too much wine and brandy, but I'll taper
off later. Who is watering my plants?
I may go home as wide as Gertrude Stein
—another Jewish Lesbian in France.

Around the sculptured Dukes of Burgundy,
androgynous monastics, faces cowled,
thrust bellies out in marble ecstasy
like child swimmers having their pigtails toweled.
Kids sang last night. A frieze of celebrants
circles the tomb, though students are in school,
while May rain drizzles on the beautiful
headlines confirming François Mitterrand's
election. We have Reagan. Why not be
another Jewish Lesbian in France?

Aspiring Heads of State are literate
here, have favorite poets, can explain
the way structuralists obliterate
a text. They read at night. They're still all men.
Now poppy-studded meadows of Provence
blazon beyond our red sardine-can car.

We hope chairpersons never ask: why are
unblushing deviants abroad on grants?
My project budget listed: Entertain
another Jewish Lesbian in France.

I meant my pithy British village neighbor
who misses old days when sorority
members could always know each other: they wore
short-back-and-sides and a collar and tie.
She did, too. Slavic eyes, all romance
beneath an Eton crop with brilliantined
finger waves, photographed at seventeen
in a dark blazer and a four-in-hand:
a glimpse of salad days that made the day for
another Jewish Lesbian in France.

Then we went on to peanuts and Campari,
she and her friend, my friend and I, and then
somehow it was nine-thirty and a hurry
to car and *carte* and a carafe of wine,
Lapin Sauté or Truite Meunière in Vence.
Convivial quartet of friends and lovers:
had anyone here dreaded any other's
tears, dawn recriminations and demands?
Emphatically not. That must have been
another Jewish Lesbian in France.

It's hard to be almost invisible.
You think you must be almost perfect too.
When your community's not sizable,
it's often a community of two,
and a dissent between communicants
is a commuter pass to the abyss.
Authorities who claim you don't exist

would sometimes find you easy to convince.
(It helps if you can talk about it to
another Jewish Lesbian in France.)

A decorated she-Academician
opines we were thought up by horny males.
No woman of equivalent position
has yet taken the wind out of her sails.
(How would her "lifelong companion" have thanked her?)
Man loving Man's *her* subject, without mention
if what they do is due to her invention
—and if I'd been her mother, I'd have spanked her.
(Perhaps in a suppressed draft *Hadrian*'s
another Jewish Lesbian in France.)

Then the advocates of Feminitude
—with dashes as their only punctuation—
explain that Reason is to be eschewed:
in the Female Subconscious lies salvation.
Suspiciously like Girlish Ignorance,
it seems a rather watery solution.
If I can't dance, it's not my revolution.
If I can't think about it, I won't dance.
So let the ranks of *Psych et Po* include
another Jewish Lesbian in France.

I wish I had been packed off to the nuns
to learn good manners, Attic Greek, and Latin.
(No public Bronx Junior High School fit all that in.)
My angsts could have been casuistic ones.
It's not my feminist inheritance
to eat roots, drink leaf broth, live in a cave,
and not even know how to misbehave
with just one vowel and five consonants.

This patchwork autodidact Anglophone's
another Jewish Lesbian in France,

following Natalie Barney, Alice B.
Toklas, Djuna Barnes, generous Bryher,
Romaine Brooks, Sylvia Beach, H. D.,
Tamara de Lempicka, Janet Flanner.
They made the best use of the circumstance
that blood and stockings often both were bluish;
(they all were white, and only Alice Jewish)
wicked sept/oct/nonagenarians.
Would it have saved Simone Weil's life to be
another Jewish Lesbian in France?

It isn't sex I mean. Sex doesn't save
anyone, except, sometimes, from boredom
(and the underpaid underclass of whoredom
is often bored at work). I have a grave
suspicion ridicule of Continence
or Chastity is one way to disparage
a woman's choice of any job but marriage.
Most of us understand what we renounce.
(This was a lunchtime pep talk I once gave
another Jewish Lesbian in France

depressed by temporary solitude
but thinking coupled bliss was dubious.)
I mean: one way to love a body viewed
as soiled and soiling existential dross
is knowing through your own experience
a like body embodying a soul
to be admirable and lovable.
That is a source that merits nourishment.
Last night despair dressed as self-loathing wooed
another Jewish Lesbian in France.

The sheet was too soft. Unwashed for three weeks,
it smelled like both of us. The sin we are
beset by is despair. I rubbed my cheeks
against the cotton, thought, I wouldn't care
if it were just *my* funk. Despair expands
to fill . . . I willed my arm: extend; hand: stroke
that sullen shoulder. In the time it took
synapse to realize abstract commands,
the shoulder's owner fell asleep. Still there
another Jewish Lesbian in France.

stared at the sickle moon above the skylight,
brooding, equally sullen, that alone
is better after all. As close as my right
foot, even my bed stops being my own.
Could I go downstairs quietly, make plans
for myself, not wake her? Who didn't undress,
slept on the couch bundled with loneliness
rather than brave that nuptial expanse
five weeks before. Another contradiction
another Jewish Lesbian in France

may reconcile more gracefully than I.
We're ill equipped to be obliging wives.
The post office and travel agency
are significant others in our lives.
Last summer I left flowers at Saint Anne's
shrine. She had daughters. One who, legends tell,
adrift, woman-companioned, shored (is still
revered) in the Camargue, her holy band's
navigatrix, Mary, calming the sea
—another Jewish Lesbian in France?

It says they lived together forty years,
Mary and Mary and Sarah (who was Black).

Unsaintly ordinary female queers,
we packed up and went separately back.
We'd shared the road with Gypsy sleeper vans
to join Sarah's procession to the shore.
Our own month-end anabasis was more
ambiguous. Among Americans
my polyglot persona disappears,
another Jewish Lesbian in France.

Coeur mis à nu in sunlight, khaki pants
I've rolled up in a beach towel so ants
and crickets from the leafage won't invade
their sweaty legs: in a loaned hermit glade
pine-redolent of New Hampshire, not France,
I disentangle from the snares I laid.
Liver-lobed mushrooms thicken in the shade,
shrubs unwrap, pinelings thrust through mulch. Noon
            slants
across my book, my chest, its lemonade
rays sticky as a seven-year-old's hands.

Gerda in the Aerie

*Then the robber girl put her arm round Gerda's neck and
slept. But Gerda was much too afraid to close her eyes.*

H. C. Andersen, "The Snow Queen"

I almost love you. I've wanted to be you
all my life. You are asleep in the straw
with my story, your arm thrown across
my neck. Under your weight, I'm awake,
prickly bladdered, listening to rooks
in the eaves. Your breath rasps,
fresher than the straw, across my face.
The texture of your skin is strange because
it's familiar. I felt vertigo,
nausea, when you touched my mouth with your
mouth, smelling of peat smoke, then
vertigo took direction. I could have dived
into your dark.
            Do you have a story?
I imagine you always here, growing
with trees, testing your daily strength,
not exemplary, necessary. Corded
shoulders protect your brown new breasts
when you take off your stained embroidered shirt.
You wrapped yourself for sleep in the soft shawl
I had unknotted. Your breasts asked, like eyes.
A girl looks at another girl's breasts
covertly, thinking, we should be alike,
we are the same kind. But we are not.
Fear tethers me to the fire. I was raised afraid
of strange men, sudden noises, groups of men
in the square, isolate men on the road.

Alone in the woods, I never was alone
before. A drunk, a tinker, a bear
that meant a man, somebody's runaway
father or brother or son, would find me
expendable landscape. I'm following
a woman, now, alone. The trees
are simply trees and let me look at them.
What would a witch do to me, or a captious
princess? What a man does to a man;
nothing to make me cringe around the trees
again. The witch knew something I should know,
but I was in a hurry.
                            Listen: worst
of all was, all along, I didn't mind.
I said I was the sinewy small girl
with tucked-up skirts, who was the general,
who made a boy eat dirt, who kept one doll
dressed as a pirate. Well, I had six
beribboned china ladies with real hair.
I asked for a new one each year. I pricked
flowers on cloth where someone else had drawn
them, with my back to the sun. I liked
doing it, it made space in my mind
smooth as cream. I used diminutives,
collected miniatures. A tiny world
was what I played at, bottle-fed and tame.
You aren't listening. You're asleep
in your adventure, which I probably
won't know, maybe take part in. I won't know
what part. And this is in my head, where I
talk like a grown-up.
                            Grandma's little girl
talked like a grown-up: wait and see; wait and see.
He was my twin self, my better brother.

That was my story, that I told myself
as puberty relentlessly divided
the tomboys from the boys. First we dress dolls,
then, confine cats, then, children
are handed over to caged children
who, every day, deck and affirm the cage.
When he laughed at me, I expected it.
When he dragged his sled to the boys' pond,
I watched, behind a tree. I could have asked
to go too. I was indulged. A girl
would be safe, playing with a band of boys,
from men. But I was happy where I was.
I listened to him whistling down the hill.
I thought about my hassock near the fire
to whose round seat my first embroidery,
maroon ground, daisies and a fleur-de-lis,
was tacked, sits still. I went in. I sat still.
So it was Kay the stranger lured away.
The woman stranger. If I find them, when I find her,
will she seize me like you did, with grubby
paws: "Nobody touch her, she's *mine*!"
A *girl* said that—you did—about a girl
—*me*. I guess you saved my life. Because
a girl said it, the danger couldn't be real.
That was what made me giggle. But it was.
I thought of something I heard from the witch.
You shut out images of what you fear:
your pupils pinhole; dilate when you're shown
what you desire. A picture of a gun
dilates men's eyes. Women's shrink. (From a niche
of crumbling mortar, you plucked your honed knife
and showed it to me shyly, like a jewel
saved for betrothal. Close to your curled hand
in warm straw, now it glistens as it sleeps.)

The image of a man—if women's eyes
contract; if they widen, shown a woman;
and men's do, too; would you have been surprised?
That means some of us fear what we desire,
and don't look at it with our entire
vision. I don't think I'm afraid of you,
though I should be, but I can't sleep, here.
I don't want to get up. What do you fear?
What do you want? Are they ever the same?
I want you to wake up and talk to me.
You're here, but you aren't really here.
Your elbow's getting heavy, like a stone
or a dead branch across my collarbone,
except it smells like you. The tiniest
shove, would you wake up? I know a game
we could play, or I could tell you a story.
You could tell one. If I turn on my side
with my back to you, your arm is around
me more lightly, a hug, and I can ride
to sleep on your lap, knees bent on your knees,
my arm over your arm under my breasts,
while your wild pets make early morning sounds.

The Robber Woman

"Listen," said the Robber Girl to Gerda, "you see that all the robbers are gone. Only my mother is left and she will soon fall asleep. Then I shall do something for you."

H. C. Andersen, "The Snow Queen"

I cuffed you into shape. I molded you
in my swelling matrix, pushed you out
into the world. I push you into the world
daily, and the labor is the same:
very like pain, unless I work at it.

As long as I sleep among thieves
you are safe in the upper air.

You kicked me from the inside long enough
when I bulged with you. I put my elbows
on what must have been your pointed butt
and watched your bony angles flying out.
I picked my load up when I'd caught my breath.

As long as I sleep among thieves
you are safe in the upper air.

I hug you and I slap you. I kiss you
and I curse you. I get your booted foot
on my scarred shins. I can still throw you down
and pick you up. Most of the time, it's play.
You knocked my knife hand and my breath out today.

As long as I sleep among thieves
you are safe in the upper air.

You cheered when your head reached my belt buckle.
Now I can't peer into your matted hair.
You lean against me. I can rest my chin
on your head, smelling unwashed child, while you
play-punch my breasts the way you always did.

As long as I sleep among thieves
you are safe in the upper air.

I always feel you in my hands, like clay.
You're oven-ready now. When you are baked
in the kiln of the world, my hands could break
what they made as accidentally
as easily as anybody's hands.

As long as I sleep among thieves
you are safe in the upper air.

You've started. I've scrubbed away your first blood.
My breasts are hard as when we nursed. I'm due.
You chose your friend; you took her for yourself
up into that cat hideout where you sleep.
I hardly wonder what you talk about.

You are safe in the upper air
to believe what a child believes:
no blow that you receive
will ever leave a scar
but the impatient care-
less clout your mother gives;
certain that if you live
another hundred years
you never will forgive
a grain of malice there.

No harm ascends the stairs
unless your mother leaves
the bedroom door ajar.
The heavy step that weaves
its twist of fear in rev-
eries of empowered love
is—do you doubt it—hers.
The clean wind strips the eaves.
You stretch to what you will dare.
No one will know what you are
as long as I sleep among thieves.

The Little Robber Girl Considers
the Wide World

Far from the steamy parlors of the north,
aspiring rooftrees soar above the hearth.
Although they splay like courtiers' coolers, swards
of undergrowth clank in the wind like swords,

like that cloisonné fencing-master's skewer
mounted to proffer towels near the shower.
Whatever I can do, I'm going to do it,
with no one to forbid it or allow it.

I washed myself and washed myself. Blue tile
speculated on the ring I stole
while mispronouncing toasts with the entire
retinue of a People's Ambassador

who pinched my arm and reeled out such a line!
It's harder work than huddling in the cold.
I'm tired of eating all my meals alone,
glimpsing myself in silver like a child.

I can salvage without being foolish:
whatever tales her scraggly carrion birds
hear from my mother as she rocks and broods,
only my ankles and my wrists are girlish.

They said I'd bake to blazes, but they lied.
I think I never will be warm enough.
The noon sun satisfies my lizard blood.
I wish I hadn't given her my knife

because she didn't cry though I could bruise
her with my thumb. She doesn't know I loathe
her drool about an ice boy and a rose.
It was like stroking a blacksnake: too smooth.

She'd tell me better secrets if I pried.
Sooner or later, I'd get tired of bossing
her around. If I could tweak and prod
her to fight back, that would be appetizing—

except she went away early this morning,
saddle-strapped like a piglet on a spit.
(I can't ride horses well yet, but I'm learning.)
Beyond the egret's marsh, I found a spot . . .

Oh, I can't even make up a good story.
I stomp around the footpath, getting bitten
by gnats and kicking rocks and feeling rotten.
I'm bored, is all: it isn't so mysteri-

ous. It's hours and hours and hours till dinner.
I wish I had my knife. I bet she'll drop
it and lose it, or give it to that drip
and never use it for herself. Piss on her!

Rune of the Finland Woman

for Sára Karig

"You are so wise," the reindeer said, "you can bind the winds of the world in a single strand."

H. C. Andersen, "The Snow Queen"

She could bind the world's winds in a single strand.
She could find the world's words in a singing wind.
She could lend a weird will to a mottled hand.
She could wind a willed word from a muddled mind.

She could wend the wild woods on a saddled hind.
She could sound a wellspring with a rowan wand.
She could bind the wolf's wounds in a swaddling band.
She could bind a banned book in a silken skin.

She could spend a world war on invaded land.
She could pound the dry roots to a kind of bread.
She could feed a road gang on invented food.
She could find the spare parts of the severed dead.

She could find the stone limbs in a waste of sand.
She could stand the pit cold with a withered lung.
She could handle bad puns in the slang she learned.
She could dandle foundlings in their mother tongue.

She could plait a child's hair with a fishbone comb.
She could tend a coal fire in the Arctic wind.
She could mend an engine with a sewing pin.
She could warm the dark feet of a dying man.

She could drink the stone soup from a doubtful well.
She could breathe the green stink of a trench latrine.
She could drink a queen's share of important wine.
She could think a few things she would never tell.

She could learn the hand code of the deaf and blind.
She could earn the iron keys of the frozen queen.
She could wander uphill with a drunken friend.
She could bind the world's winds in a single strand.

The Little Robber Girl Gets On in
the Wide World

for Julie Fay

She's in a room full of letters, dressed in white
amidst proliferate papers, the exploded lace of sheets.
Her hair froths white, her pale eyes chill, as when I first
saw her. Under white trouser legs, her long feet

are bare on the stone floor, swollen with heat.
Summer follows summer since the first time
I stood in her crepuscular bedroom
awaiting acknowledgment. The dim chime

of a blue glass clock caught her attention. "I'm
exhausted. Come at six tomorrow. Knock
downstairs. I'll hear you. The heat makes me sick.
Debarrass me of that ridiculous clock."

I put it in my pocket. I left the lock
unlatched. Who knows what I thought I'd do?
I watched from a huge-boled olive tree, her window
a tall candle, while dusk deepened, blue

as my road clothes, and a blade of new
moon sharpened above the limestone bluffs.
"I knew where you were last night. I heard you laugh."
Her sight is dim, but her ears are sharp enough.

I thought, "Let her be captious, she's a tough
old bird, and, say what you like, she deserves

a bit of courtesy. While I'm here, I won't starve.
You're not a slave when you contract to serve."

I don't know when it was I lost my nerve.
I was delighted when she seemed to trust
me. I brought the right coins back, her birdscratch list
transformed to fill the larder. Late in the August

heat, shadowed by shutters, we discussed
my future and her past. Sometimes they blended
to one chivalric tale. I understand it
a little better now. She would make splendid

generous gestures in which I pretended
to believe. If it were hers to give,
she'd give it to me—what? her land, her glove
to carry, the bracelet under her sleeve?

Pretended? Why? She didn't want me to leave;
she told me so in several languages,
while I continued to sleep under her trees,
presenting myself mornings, neatly dressed

as I could manage. Each day was a new test.
She sent me out and always I came back
with packages, messages. "You bring me good luck."
I had good luck, I thought. I had a knack

for pleasing. The blue glass clock lived in my rucksack.
Afternoons, I wrote letters, a diligent steward,
weeded the moribund garden while it parched,
stood barefoot on cool tiles while she descended

the tortuous stairway, her gnarled hand extended
toward me. Did I say, she was beautiful,
that youth, in her scintillant pallor, paled
to decorative nursery pastel?

I felt large, rude and bland, all the more grateful,
though my food and outdoor shelter were all my wages.
Blackberry clumps weighted the brambly hedges.
Sometimes I thought of winter hills' blank pages

scrawled with one bird track. I forgot my real age—is
that strange? and that once I was almost always cold.
Brown rabbits and gray water rats ran wild
in the hedges. No animal should be killed

on her land, she said. My nights outdoors were filled
with rustlings, scrabblings. I thought about rats
and rolled down, shivering, into my blankets.
"Womanish," she mocked, when I told her that.

I plunged my face into a fresh-washed sheet
as I lifted it to hang. The odor
of wet linen enveloped unthought-of tears.
I never had done woman's work before

but now I did it daily, over and over.
Sometimes I was insulted, as no servant
who'd take her pay and leave would be. I didn't.
Sometimes I was her twilight confidante,

gallant, or granddaughter, or sycophant.
She liked me best when I was brusque and lewd.
If I was timid, she would call me stupid,
but she'd laugh and correct a misconstrued

sentence I almost halfway understood.
The sun set earlier, but we sat late. Around her
shoulders, I wrapped her black-barred cloak. She was
    fonder
of talk than fire. Meanwhile the magpies, sometimes the
    thunder,

meanwhile the footpath wound serpentine under
the bushes, tucked in around limestone boulders
above the river-sectioned slopes where wilder
things wandered in the night as I got older,

and she, chameleon, stayed the same, I told her.
Meanwhile the trail debouched on a small road
that led—although I didn't know where it led—
somewhere. From our hill, it was hidden by woods.

After a storm, mist marked the bluffs: it showed.
Meanwhile I scrabbled weeds where no one reaped.
Harvest was windfall. Greengages the wasps
ate splattered tree roots, or heaped

in their forks, a rats' feast while we slept.
Smashed yellow pears fermented in the grass
the afternoon I thought I'd cut my losses.
With a soiled shirt sleeve, I rubbed the milk-glass

clock till my face glimmered back from its facets.
I wrapped my four garments around it, rolled
them in my blanket. I stripped her down-drowned bed
of its Champagne-silk crewelwork. I sold

that to a market woman. Well, I thought of it, told
myself I ought, might, was entitled to,

as I tied up the rucksack. *Do you know,*
that's probably what she expects of you?

So I turn, part hedges, shield my eyes. I go
up to my haunches in persistent brambles.
Nobody promised me it would be simple.
Nobody's future passes out free samples.

Sunbeams stroked me at a farewell angle
while the watchlight in my mind's eye sought her
shadow smiting rock with an olive crosier:
"You are a thief, and a thief's daughter!"

Ballad of Ladies Lost and Found

for Julia Álvarez

Where are the women who, *entre deux guerres*,
came out on college-graduation trips,
came to New York on football scholarships,
came to town meeting in a decorous pair?
Where are the expatriate *salonnières*,
the gym teacher, the math-department head?
Do nieces follow where their odd aunts led?
The elephants die off in Cagnes-sur-Mer.
H. D., whose "nature was bisexual,"
and plain old Margaret Fuller died as well.

Where are the single-combat champions:
the Chevalier d'Eon with curled peruke,
Big Sweet who ran with Zora in the jook,
open-handed Winifred Ellerman,
Colette, who hedged her bets and always won?
Sojourner's sojourned where she need not pack
decades of whitegirl conscience on her back.
The spirit gave up Zora; she lay down
under a weed field miles from Eatonville,
and plain old Margaret Fuller died as well.

Where's Stevie, with her pleated schoolgirl dresses,
and Rosa, with her permit to wear pants?
Who snuffed Clara's *mestiza* flamboyance
and bled Frida onto her canvases?
Where are the Niggerati hostesses,
the kohl-eyed ivory poets with severe

chignons, the rebels who grew out their hair,
the bulldaggers with marceled processes?
Conglomerates co-opted Sugar Hill,
and plain old Margaret Fuller died as well.

Anne Hutchinson, called witch, termagant, whore,
fell to the long knives, having tricked the noose.
Carolina María de Jesús'
tale from the slag heaps of the landless poor
ended on a straw mat on a dirt floor.
In action thirteen years after fifteen
in prison, Eleanor of Aquitaine
accomplished half of Europe and fourscore
anniversaries for good or ill,
and plain old Margaret Fuller died as well.

Has Ida B. persuaded Susan B.
to pool resources for a joint campaign?
(Two Harriets act a pageant by Lorraine,
cheered by the butch drunk on the IRT
who used to watch me watch her watching me.)
We've notes by Angelina Grimké Weld
for choral settings drawn from the *Compiled
Poems* of Angelina Weld Grimké.
There's no such tense as Past Conditional,
and plain old Margaret Fuller died as well.

Who was Sappho's protégée, and when did
we lose Hrotsvitha, dramaturge and nun?
What did bibulous Suzanne Valadon
think about Artemisia, who tended
to make a life-size murderess look splendid?
Where's Aphra, fond of dalliance and the pun?
Where's Jane, who didn't indulge in either one?

Whoever knows how Ende, Pintrix, ended
is not teaching Art History at Yale,
and plain old Margaret Fuller died as well.

Is Beruliah upstairs behind the curtain
debating Juana Inés de la Cruz?
Where's savante Anabella, Augusta-Goose,
Fanny, Maude, Lidian, Freda and Caitlin,
"without whom this could never have been written"?
Louisa who wrote, scrimped, saved, sewed, and nursed,
Malinche, who's, like all translators, cursed,
Bessie, whose voice was hemp and steel and satin,
outside a segregated hospital,
and plain old Margaret Fuller died as well.

Where's Amy, who kept Ada in cigars
and love, requited, both country and courtly,
although quinquagenarian and portly?
Where's Emily? It's very still upstairs.
Where's Billie, whose strange fruit ripened in bars?
Where's the street-scavenging Little Sparrow?
Too poor, too mean, too weird, too wide, too narrow:
Marie Curie, examining her scars,
was not particularly beautiful;
and plain old Margaret Fuller died as well.

Who was the grandmother of Frankenstein?
The Vindicatrix of the Rights of Woman.
Madame de Sévigné said prayers to summon
the postman just as eloquent as mine,
though my Madame de Grignan's only nine.
But Mary Wollstonecraft had never known
that daughter, nor did Paula Modersohn.
The three-day infants blinked in the sunshine.

The mothers turned their faces to the wall;
and plain old Margaret Fuller died as well.

Tomorrow night the harvest moon will wane
that's floodlighting the silhouetted wood.
Make your own footnotes; it will do you good.
Emeritae have nothing to explain.
She wasn't very old, or really plain—
my age exactly, volumes incomplete.
"The life, the life, will it never be sweet?"
She wrote it once; I quote it once again
midlife at midnight when the moon is full
and I can almost hear the warning bell
offshore, sounding through starlight like a stain
on waves that heaved over what she began
and truncated a woman's chronicle,
and plain old Margaret Fuller died as well.

GOING BACK TO THE RIVER

1 9 9 0

Two Cities

I
The streetlights bent
the sleet streams as I went
up the deserted rue des Deux-Ponts,

the only one
except two boy drunks on
the steep slope of rue Cardinal-Lemoine.

I took the sharp
turn toward the Place de la Contrescarpe.
Firelight shimmered in the rain. A group

of tramps, five men,
two women, warmed their hands
over an open fire in an oil drum.

Rain beat down hard.
A bear-man with a beard
passed the glistening bottle of *pinard*

to an old one,
who tipped it. Her red cheeks shone
like a child's, come in from the sun.

I had both your
keys for the rue Tournefort,
and my own, for back across the river.

It cleared my head
when I walked from desk to bed,
rive droite, rive gauche, the distance I needed.

That "worst winter
in decades," crossing the center
of Paris, I was the inventor

of my own life,
an old plane tree in new leaf,
a young woman almost forty-five.

                              II

When I was sick
I stayed under the thick
couch cover, with the electric

fire on three bars,
drapes pulled to muffle cars
and buses passing, a sweatshirt (yours)

keeping my arms
warm while I read. A rainstorm
chewed on last night's snow; a fire alarm

ripped the thick air
outside, not my interior
weather. Earl Grey with milk. Dusk fell at four-

thirty. Neighbors
pulling shopping carts upstairs
stopped with the ninety-year-old next door

eager to un-
latch for the rue Saint-Antoine
gossip with her evening bread and wine.

Tiny, bird-boned,
daily she'd done her own
errands, seven decades living alone,

until she slipped
on iced stairs and cracked her hip.
She wants the food less than the gossip.

Hands round my cup,
I thought how you'd come up-
stairs too in three hours. We'd cut bread, ladle soup,

pour wine, refill
the glasses for my cold, your chilled
hands, lie down to sleep together until

her radio
at six A.M. let us know
the night had come and gone next door also.

III

The carrot-top
above the Mom-and-Pop
hardware shook out her dust mop,

a cigarette
in her mouth. Three years, I'd yet
to see her dressed. She slapped a small carpet

on the worked rail,
square in a square nightshirt. The trail
of dust and ashes floated past the mail

truck, sun-yellow,
leg up on the curb, pillowed
on grimy snow. In the window below,

a gray woman
checked what the shoppers had on
and buttoned up a black cardigan.

Two boys, short pants,
school satchels on their backs, danced
with cold at the bus stop, rubbing their hands.

In the dormer
window of the former
maid's room, chinked rags kept somebody warmer.

A flock of gray
clouds at roof peak skirled away.
The blue banner of a windy day

unfurled while I
poured a fresh cup of coffee
laced with hot milk, and sat and watched it fly.

IV

Nine months later,
on a terrace with my daughter,
eating *moules*, we saw the blue-jeaned waiter

abruptly turn
his gorgeous Euro-African
profile toward upper Broadway, where a young,

or not young, blonde
cursed out the night around
her, and someone who'd knocked her down.

Drunk? Crack? Her mind?
She slashed in front, behind
herself with a slim cane. "I think she's blind!"

Iva whispered
as the woman disappeared
past the balcony. As if she'd heard,

she turned, came back,
cheeks slack, gray anorak
in September, brandishing her stick.

She lunged with it
and raked the table opposite
us. Plates crashed, glass shattered. "Damn you, you shit!"

addressed to no
one specific. When you know
the words so well, they're not vivid argot,

only despair,
as the beautiful waiter
vaulted the rail, pinioned her there

till the cop van
came. The couple got free wine
at a fresh table while the floor was cleaned.

Nights of 1962: The River Merchant's Wife

for Carol Lee Hane

Émigrée from the Bronx, a married child
hit the ghetto-turned-barrio, making wild
conjectures and conjunctions, making wrong
turns on lyrics of country-and-western songs.
Moondark to dawn, loud streets were not-quite-scary
footnotes in a nocturnal dictionary
of argot softer on my ears than known
four-walled cadenzas to: the night alone,
the day on fire. (My age, the boss boy knew.)
From Avenue C west to Sixth Avenue
and Eighth Street, I'd aim for the all-night Whelan's,
eat solo ham and eggs. The night sky paled, sands
into the river's timer. One more day:
jeans switched for dark dress, tight shoes, the subway
to work at Altman's. Five months short of twenty,
I knocked back whatever the river sent. He
was gone two days; might bring back, on the third,
some kind of night music I'd never heard:
Sonny the burglar, paunched with breakfast beers;
olive-skinned Simon, who made fake Vermeers;
the cardsharp who worked club cars down the coast;
Carol, stone butch, who'd booked Chip's group, was host,
bouncer, bookkeeper, and night manager
of a folk club. The night she spotted her
sometime girlfriend naked in my red chalk
drawings taped to the john wall, we had a talk
about how she bridged night's work and day's work,
a dude till dawn, a nine-to-five file clerk

in heels and hose. Some grass: she demonstrated
her butch walk, girl walk, paced, like a five-gaited
horse, the splintered floor, miming her cross-
over from flunky to three A.M. yard boss.
Fox-faced in burnt sienna, the judge's daughter
ignored us. Was it Carol who had bought her
the watch she left on, posing, to keep time?
I learned the lesson as a paradigm
of living day-life, night-life, Janus-faced.
Why didn't Carol, older, have her own place?
Where did she sleep the nights she didn't crash
on our spare mattress at East Fifth Street? Cash
she stored in the front pocket of her drip-
dry chinos, which she slept *on*, laid out under
the mattress for their knife edge. Who, I wondered,
did she sleep *with*, now? She'd told things to Chip
she wouldn't tell me, who'd only (she'd guess) botched
stoned fumblings while somebody's boyfriend watched.
I knew the boys' bars—did she go to one
for girls? I dawdled nights on the question.
Two weeks later: what did they make of me
on a barstool at the Sea Colony
in a paint-splattered Black Watch shirt, old khak-
i work pants, one long braid straight down my back,
chain-smoking Camels, making my second Bud
last? I sipped it as slowly as I could,
looking around me surreptitiously.
Boys' bars had dance floors. Puerto Rican queens
in mohair sweaters, who'd worked up routines
in kitchens, line-danced to "No Milk Today,"
"From a Jack to a Queen," "Walk Like a Man,"
too cool to giggle at the double enten-
dres, cruising without seeming to cruise.
No one was dancing here. Women in twos,

each suit-and-tie paired with a plunge-necked sheath,
held hands at tiny tables, closed. Bad teeth
and Brooklyn accents, nineteen-year-old snob
thought, in the wrong outfit for either job
—and how invade with chat hermetically
sealed couples? Somebody romantically
forty-plus, foreign, solitary, face
defined by facing danger, in this place
for R&R, who'd like my mind, whose bed,
dovetailed by bookshelves, was four blocks away . . .
Seduction by the French Department head
to whom I owed a paper on Genet
was what I had in mind, and I assumed
she'd know how to proceed beyond the full-
face closeup kiss on which my mind's lens zoomed
in, blanked out. I should have followed Carol
on her night off. She knew the regulars,
I guessed. I couldn't sit on a barstool
reading, till closing. Chip had adventures;
I, it seemed, had trepidations. Full
of them, I got down the rest of my beer
and turned tail, out the door into the night
streets, which aroused just reasonable fear.
I lengthened my strides streetlight to streetlight,
in no hurry to regain the empty
conjugal crash pad and wait out the dregs
of the dark. I was, I told myself, hungry
enough to hit Whelan's for ham and eggs.

April Interval

Wherever I surface I reinvent
some version of the Daily Walk to Town:
two miles rewarded with an hour's browse round
the market square or its equivalent:
a yard sale off the Dyer County Road,
Rua Visconde de Pirajá.
Company is unwanted as a car.
I have, I've found, an operative code.
Perhaps, at forty, I'm escaping Nurse
Conscience to look for Mother in the shops;
perhaps irregularities, slow stops,
burst-starts of footfall echo feats of verse.
Perhaps it's just that I procrastinate
incorrigibly, as I've always done,
justified by a footpath splashed with sun.
Precipitation is precipitate.
Now I'm an orphaned spinster with a home
where spoils of these diurnal expeditions
can be displayed in prominent positions.
I'll hang this crazy quilt in the front room,
its unembarrassedly polychrome
velvet rhomboids and uneven satin
patches lined with fancywork, no pattern
twice. She painted flowers and leaves on some
a hundred years ago. I know it's "she."
"The life," at my age, will only be "sweet"
as I make it. I can't guarantee
myself a Boston marriage or more money,
but I can be outdoors and on my feet
as long as I'm still sound, and it's still sunny.

Riposte

(I never could
Figure out how anyone can justify poetry
As a full-time job. How do they get through
The day at MacDowell—filling out
Applications for the next free lunch?)

Tom Disch, "Working on a Tan"

Dear Tom,
     When my next volume (granted: slender)
is granted an advance of more than two
thou, perhaps I'll scorn all grants and spend a
couple of them on summer rent, like you,

in the right Hampton with the novelists
who swap Hollywood options with bravado.
Their au pairs hoard handwritten shopping lists;
their word processors go with them to Yaddo

where novelists are still persona grata,
nor do their royalties or last advance
cause the per diem charge to rise pro rata.
I'd ever so much rather be in France

and not have to eat dinner at six-thirty
with frozen carrots and Kraft's French *(sic)* Dressing.
But potshotting "free lunch" is playing dirty;
successful applicants should count their blessings.

I wouldn't want the kitchen staff to brand me
an ingrate who will bite the hand that feeds me
if I am going to eat the food they hand me
—and they're in the minority that reads me.

Is poetry a full-time occupation?
Practitioners have spliced it with exciting
alternative careers in transportation
—drive cabs, that is—or teach Creative Writing

or First Year French or Freshman Composition,
translate, wait tables, sell insurance, edit.
If "poet" 's written where it says: PROFESSION:
American Express extends no credit.

And you see no excuse for poets' lives
because we're paid so mingily; that's it?
I think of "unemployed" mothers, housewives
whose work was judged equivalent to shit

shoveling on Frank Perdue's chicken farm
by gents who calibrate Job Equity.
All that they are today they owe to Mom!
Do novelists owe shit to poetry?

SF writer snipes poets on the pages
of *Poetry:* that's also aiming low,
though nowhere near as low as poets' wages.
At fifty cents a line, where would *you* go?

And fifty cents a line's exemplary!
Measure it to your last *Playboy* short-short
and you might find an artists' colony
a perfectly respectable resort.

Late August Letter

for Eavan Boland

Dear Eavan,
Just yesterday afternoon
in my notebook I'd written
your letter on my wish list
for August. On Assumption

your round hand
was under the Eire stamp and
salmon-turquoise Airmail band
on the mail table. Sprung from
the boredom of boarders' bland

school dinners
where the chosen word spinners,
shape makers mind their manners,
I felt like a local track
maverick who'd picked winners.

On the free-
way outside the colony
mill rugose beef-bloat poly-
acrylic American
racing fans. From family

armored cars
they haul flattened web lawn chairs,
inevitable coolers
of beer they truck through the dust
for the thirst they'll rouse with cheers.

Half past ten,
the streets are silent again.
No women gossip, no men
play cards. From each house I walk
past glares chalk television

light: canned voices
recorded sometime/where else.
No children are making noise.
Through the black trees, one dimmed star.
From their car, out-of-town boys,

holiday
drunk, cruise for something to lay.
(Ten bars: one is "sort of gay.")
I cross; they drive on, no hass-
le, I pass—passed as a boy?

Dawn: racecourse
misted, glimpsed totemic horse
shapes incarnate grace's force.
One leans on his girl groom's knee
being refreshed with a hose.

Children ex-
ercise them mornings at six.
She, arrowed from her mount's neck's
thundering into the sky.
I walk by, cracking dry sticks

underfoot
in the hoofprinted mud, out
before coffee—none until eight!
I measure distance enough
to stave off my caffeine fit.

Breakfast's on
in the art nouveau mansion
turned, in one generation,
hothouse for artists' labors.
My neighbor's Nigerian—

he's "the one."
Whitefolk are almost legion
(and childed single women).
One Black woman novelist
left the rest to eat alone

every day
in West House. Her grocery
bags were tagged in the pantry.
Weeks, and I never met her.
(Another woman told me.)

I'm the queer
apple in the barrel here.
A playwright-novelist pair
may be indulging in a
Claudine à l'école affair—

but I'm just
as contented to be chaste,
though quite cognizant that last
statement may appear to be
irony by April first.

In Ireland
—where the midsummer high ground
of your talk excited wan-
derlust in me to be—how
are you now, what work's at hand?

I haven't
said, but I do imagine
the peaks of conversation
we might scale if I were there,
or you nearby, dear Eavan.

Country & Western

She will never know I cried for her
in a motel outside Memphis, far
west as you go in the East. By TV light
—Clark Gable hunted the last mustangs down
while Marilyn Monroe wept in the pickup—
Julie smoked in bed, restless, a headache

coming on, as my two-day headache
receded, and the rain steamed dry. In her
Toyota, we'd come a thousand miles. She'd pick up
her bloke in Phoenix, come from Nice, a far
cry from where she'd packed the car: a down
vest for the Rockies, Coleman stove, flashlight,

tent, lantern, three months' books. I traveled light,
along for a week's driving, a headach-
y novice. At the river, rain sluiced down
the windshield. Julie drank Wild Turkey from her
plastic flask. Teenagers in a pickup
tossed beer cans, almost visible, as far

as the riverbank erased by rain. We'd fore-
cast storms: no wet camping. When torrents light-
ened up, we struck the tent. I'd have tried to pick up
the blond girl Ranger, but my headache
throbbed: nothing else could. While I talked to her
I hurt. We thought *she* thought she had us down

as lovers when she said which motel down
the road would have us: Northern women, for-
eigners. She'd *one* red fingernail; beneath her

Hawaiian shirt, a gold cross. In the last light
we drove off, checked in. I left my headache
in the Montana Bar. Steaks, beer: when I pick up

a glass, a fork, I know my mood will pick up
too, and it did, till, later, I lay down
on that square hired bed. She was in my head: ache
in a severed part a thousand miles weren't far
enough to salve. She'd pick that film, her Lite
beside the bed. Not Julie, not the Ranger: her

hand not far from her crotch, blond head near my head,
      ach-
ing back I'd pound; she'd pick up, then put down
the beer . . . I doused the light. I cried for her.

Country & Western II

It looks like we are the Last Unmarried
Women in Tucson. We talk about food,
drinking, and mountains. They talk about babies.
We're going to have to go outside to smoke.
Is there any more bourbon in the car?
It's too early to want to go to bed

in sleeping bags *indoors.* Fun in bed
in Tucson happens after you get married
—why every teenager has got a car.
As Carol peeled and chopped, we talked about food
we'd cooked at campsites: *mole con* charcoal smoke
for two nights running. She talked about babies

and I remembered talking about babies
incessantly, when I had one, in bed
in a basket under my desk. I'd smoke,
swill coffee, and discuss her. I stayed married
for nine months after that. We talk about food
in the morning, while you waltz the car

around the mall, for space next to a car
bigger enough to vouchsafe shade (a BABY's
ON BOARD, decals announce). We talk about food
on down the Giant's twelve aisles, each one a Bed
of Procrustes. Do you *want* to get married,
and why? There's fire, but you've had all that smoke

in your eyes before. If I could smoke
dope without crashing, I'd say, let's take the car

up one of your mountains. Sunset married
to sky, we'd gaze, get high. If Carol's baby-
sitter showed up, Carol would come—but her bed-
and-board mate would get home and want his food.

O even gorged with cheap Mexican food,
the counterculture, rounding forty (smoke
defiantly, hint an unlicensed bed
or two, have drinking buddies now incar-
cerated), still had curfews: home to babies.
"A toast, first, to these two, who just got married!"

(The rest, like me, married when they were babies.)
Before bedtime, we'll toast your yellow car,
smoke while we watch the stars, and talk about food.

Letter from Goose Creek: April

for K. J.

We're both in Greenville, but a state apart.
About the time you were due to arrive,
I was helping Julie stack wood for the stove.
There was frost last night. When we had to start
the fire up, I remembered you, me, and the dog
sprawled out on the brown-and-gold rag rug
as you wedged twigs and kindling till the log
caught; then you and I kindled from a hug
while the fire blazed, from slow afternoon's talking.
Bright afternoon here now, through which I drove
two lanes at a journeyman's fifty-five
thirty miles to Goose Creek from the Kmart
—smooth starts at traffic lights are still the worst part.
What changes nothing changes everything.

There are no detours circumventing grief.
The spare-room pillow's littered with the "Tracks
Of My Tears" again. I came unstuck
at dawn when gray light off-printed oak-leaf
shapes, vague as clouds before; and then, my eyes
hopelessly open, I pulled last night's clothes
back on. Outside the window, three outsize
woodpeckers in the feeder and a rose-
breasted she-cardinal were bickering
while I rattled round Julie's kitchen, look-
ing for the coffeepot. The falling back's
inevitable. I know you know brief
descents yourself. Juice, coffee, and relief.
What changes nothing changes everything.

You were the friend who got me through the night
I packed her things. It was a few nights after,
when, stuck on upper Broadway in your car
with postal sacks you'd ferried me to get,
"Was I a good friend or an inadequate
lover?" you asked, about our friend, who'd died
with you, months vigilant by her bedside,
years warily defining why and what
you couldn't. Then the wind had you, raging
your mourning across a continent we were
sometimes conjoined by, like the curiouser
fossils. From my stratum, trilobite
dislodged, bordering yours, I did what might
have changed nothing, or changes everything.

Cold rain sheeted the Long Island Expressway
the Ides of March, commuters on our necks.
We were, I noticed, talking about sex
in a half gossip, half "I should confess . . ." way.
I know I thought, "I wonder where this gets
us, in the rain, stuck indoors on our butts
days, at the edge of nowhere?" I said, "Let's,"
eventually. Trust me: it took guts
even in the dark, and in the dark, and in the morning,
a new diplomacy to hold the checks
and balances of night, which brought the next
night's badges of courage. I undressed, lay
down with you, until our hands found the best way,
changing nothing, of changing everything.

There isn't question of an instant replay.
The past hasn't sufficiently gone past
for that to be in either's interest.
Still, in the night beside you, I could sleep; stay

sane through a blighted anniversary
walking beside the water in daylight.
I didn't think of her when you touched me,
though she brought my insomnia last night
and in the live oaks is a lingering
absence. While you're being a houseguest
inland, I try, near the Atlantic coast,
something you taught me well enough to keep—see
that something in you touched something in me deeply.
What changes nothing changes everything.

How many states and interstates and cities
will find us, our miles and our trajectories
between us, both maneuvering strange keys
to borrowed rooms? Some faculty committees
will host me while your wanderlust hosts you
from friend to friend, vistas you never saw
before, to mornings with completely new
prospects, suggesting that you stay or go
on: suddenly an interesting
itinerary on the map of raw
absence. If you weren't young till now,
now's the time. Reading the highways
between the lines, you're geared, you're gone. The key's
what changes. Nothing changes everything.

This morning I sent you a postcard of
East Carolina University.
You need to learn disponibility.
I yearn to feel I'm central where I love.
That's a difference. Friendships survive, can thrive
on differences. Yours and mine has. Julie and I've
lived ours. A beach walk followed a midday drive.
Sheltered by boulders, with the dog, beside

the Sound in sunlight, you and I made spring
welcome. Because we did, it is today
welcome still, on the live oak trail, while Julie
reads Cather on a deck chair in the cove.
What's possible is possible: enough
that change is: that one thing changes everything.

Nights of 1964–1966: The Old Reliable

for Lewis Ellingham

The laughing soldiers fought to their defeat . . .
James Fenton, "In a Notebook"

White decorators interested in Art,
Black file clerks with theatrical ambitions,
kids making pharmaceutical revisions
in journals Comp. instructors urged they start,
the part-Cherokee teenage genius (maybe),
the secretary who hung out with fairies,
the copywriter wanting to know, where is
my husband? the soprano with the baby,
all drank draft beer or lethal sweet Manhattans
or improvised concoctions with tequila
in summer when, from Third Street, we could feel a
night breeze waft in whose fragrances were Latin.
The place was run by Polish refugees:
squat Margie, gaunt Speedy (whose sobriquet
transliterated what?). He'd brought his play
from Łódź. After a while, we guessed Margie's
illiteracy was why *he* cashed checks
and *she* perched near the threshold to ban pros,
the underage, the fugitive, and those
arrayed impertinently to their sex.
The bar was talk and cruising; in the back
room, we danced: Martha and the Vandellas,
Smokey and the Miracles, while sellers
and buyers changed crisp tens for smoke and smack.
Some came in after work, some after supper,
plumage replenished to meet who knew who.
Behind the bar, Margie dished up beef stew.

On weeknights, you could always find an upper
to speed you to your desk, and drink till four.
Loosened by booze, we drifted, on the ripples
of Motown, home in new couples, or triples,
were back at dusk, with IDs, at the door.
Bill was my roommate, Russell drank with me,
although they were a dozen years my seniors.
I walked off with the eighteen-year-old genius
—an Older Woman, barely twenty-three.
Link was new as Rimbaud, and better looking,
North Beach bar *paideon* of doomed Jack Spicer,
like Russell, our two-meter artificer,
a Corvo whose *ecclesia* was cooking.
Bill and Russell were painters. Bill had been
a monk in Kyoto. Stoned, we sketched together,
till he discovered poppers and black leather
and Zen consented to new discipline.
We shared my Sixth Street flat with a morose
cat, an arch cat, and pot plants we pruned daily.
His boyfriend had left him for an Israeli
dancer; my husband was on Mykonos.
Russell loved Harold, who was Black and bad,
and lavished on him dinners "meant for men"
like Escoffier and Brillat-Savarin.
Staunch blond Dora made rice. When she had
tucked in the twins, six flights of tenement
stairs they'd descend, elevenish, and stroll
down Third Street, desultory night patrol
gone mauve and green under the virulent
streetlights, to the bar, where Bill and I
(if we'd not come to dinner), Link, and Lew,
and Betty had already had a few.
One sweat-soaked night in pitiless July,
wedged on booth benches of cracked Naugahyde,

we planned a literary magazine
where North Beach met the Lower East Side Scene.
We could have titled it *When Worlds Collide*.
Dora was gone, "In case the children wake up."
Link lightly had decamped with someone else
(the German engineer? Or was he Bill's?).
Russell's stooped *vale* brushed my absent makeup.
Armed children spared us home, our good-night hugs
laissez-passer. We railed against the war.
Soon, some of us bused south with SNCC and CORE.
Soon, some of us got busted dealing drugs.
The file clerks took exams and forged ahead.
The decorators' kitchens blazed persimmon.
The secretary started kissing women,
and so did I, and my three friends are dead.

Elevens

There is one story and one story only . . .
Robert Graves, "To Juan at the Winter Solstice"

James A. Wright, my difficult older brother,
I'm in an airplane over your Ohio.
Twice a week, there and back, I make this journey
to Cincinnati.

You are six books I own and two I borrowed.
I'm the songs about the drunk on the runway
and leaving your lover for the airport, first
thing in the morning.

You were fifty-two when you died of cancer
of the tongue, apologist for the lonely
girls who were happened to near some bleak water.
Tell me about it.

When my father died young, my mother lost it.
I am only three years younger than he was.
The older brother and the younger brother
that I never had

died young, in foreign cities, uncomforted.
Does anybody not die uncomforted?
My friend Sonny had her lovers around her
and she died also.

Half drunk on sunlight in my second country,
I yearned through six-line stanzas I learned from you.
You spent January of your last winter
up on that mountain.

I love a boy who died and a girl who left.
I love a brother who is a grown woman.
I love your eight books. I hate the ending.
I never knew you.

You knew a lot about airports and rivers
and a girl who went away in October.
Fathers, brothers and sisters die of cancer:
still, we are strangers.

You are the lonely gathering of rivers
below the plane that left you in Ohio;
you are the fog of language on Manhattan
where it's descending.

Late August

The weather is changing. The mountainous temperate
    climate
edges toward autumn.
There's a crowded sound in the rattling leaves of the fig tree
and I think of cities,
though the second fruit, ovarian, purple, splitting to scarlet
is ready for picking.
The brambles hedging pink villas banked up from the
    roadway
burgeon with berries
ripening black, seeded, sweet, which the French don't
    bother to gather,
but sometimes I do,
taking an extra plastic bag in my back pocket, coming
up from the market.
I'm less often tempted to strip off my shirt in the morning
at work on the terrace.
The bedsheets are grimy and wrinkled, but why should
    we haul
to the costly laundry
what we'd need for a couple of days? All our conversations
touch on departure.

Dear Jool,
I Miss You in
Saint-Saturnin

You mocked me that hot day at Carcassonne,
"We're *tourists* now!" waving the green Michelin.
We'd come to meet your old pals from Tucson—

yards tall, blond, Woolrich-trousered, Aryan.
They wanted dinner well before sunset,
and, sure enough, they were vegetarian,

so I negotiated them an omelette
someplace where we could have our cassoulet.
You'd hiked loved hills with her, as dry and hot

as the autoroute you drove all day
to bring old friend and newer one together.
Home was just a postal code away

a village on a hilltop we would rather
the Michelin never noticed. For a while,
home. You came there first with Jean, your mother,

after a voyage meant to reconcile
whom adolescence and divorce divided.
Her white dress plunged to suntanned back, a style

you'd never wear, but picked for her. Your pride did
show, and she mirrored it. I'd been alone,
felt like an orphan, though I tried to hide it.

Then, with my daughter and your mother gone,
you tacked your work sheets to your bedroom walls.
We shaped our hours to work and silence, nun-

like, we thought. Wind chimed matins, and birdcalls
vespers that pealed us to the kitchen where
we cooked our day's rewards. The waterfalls

near Mas Audran were yours, the vineyards were
mine—to walk around. The air was gold
with broom, and grape-leaf, plane-tree green, the air

was blue blue blue July. With wine, we told
each other that we'd be old ladies on
a hill like this, where people still got old

in housedresses and navy cardigans
or patriotic azure *salopettes.*
We'd gossip French and write American.

Our vegetarian compatriates
caught us up on reviews, tenure, careers
and marriages. We smoked French cigarettes

and ordered brandy. They had two more beers.
I stacked ashes around my coffee cup, ill
with sociability. Maverick queer,

maverick straight: two singles to their couple:
I'm sure that the comparison occurred
to both of us. We found the going uphill

worth it, if our hill was the vineyard-
and-orchard-covered slope we'd reascend
laden with *cèpes* and *confit de canard.*

That was three years ago this month. I send
this from one of the wine-veined valley towns
that shone like firefly cages at the end

of day from our roof terrace. Dusk around
them glowed. We called them "Cities of the Plain"
because it was unsuitable, choked down

our drinks guessing what might be mortal sin
to garrulous hard-working villagers.
We hoped it had to do with doctored wine.

My love is here and mine and I am hers.
Iva is elsewhere, utterly thirteen.
Jean could have told me, "Daughters!" And
          mothers . . .

This ought to be an elegy for Jean
who came back on last furlough from what grew
in her, from pain, to see you fitted in

the satin gown she wore at twenty-two.
This should be an epithalamium,
but is for solitudes shared in the blue

vat of Meridional air: for you.

Le Travail Rajeunit

Lace cushions were considered by a tall
Martiniquaise;
an Arab housewife (they go out Fridays)
plucked up and measured a divided
skirt. Five cartons, dwarfed by wheeled stalls:

"Everything's to be sold!
Children's clothes? Go through
the boxes. Boy or girl? What size are you
looking for? The paintings I did
myself. I'm eighty-six years old.

"I never saw an art school.
Would this fit
your little girl?" "It's exquisite,
but she's too tall." From her slat-sided
barrow, the fruit seller: "You'll

strain your eyes." "It's no strain."
"Do you paint at night?"
The *charcutière* leaned down in her white
stained smock. Glistening forearms collided
with hung hams. Knobbly cane

raised, the painter pushed back her straw hat.
"Never! Mornings
I put a paper block out with the breakfast things.
I set my paints beside it.
I work two hours like that."

Fists in the pockets of her blue
apron, the fruiterer
came round the stand to have a look at her
clipper ships. "*Chouette!* I've never tried it,
but it must be hard to do!"

"Your grandchildren will see them
years from now. 'An eighty-six-
year-old woman, self-taught, from the sticks
of Gignac did these,' they'll say on the guided
tours in the museum!

"My grandson's an architect. He's had
bad luck. He's out of work
a year now. Are there jobs in—you're from Belgium?—
        New York?
I sell these to help him through." (Why did
they have to be so bad?)

Someone's toddler pushed past my legs
so she could see
one board: Black *abeng* player under palm tree.
The island woman eyed it
too; then she joined the queue for eggs.

Languedocienne

for K. J.

This morning the wind came, shaking the quince tree,
making trouble in the chicken yard.

The attic door blew open, windows slammed their
        casements,
notebooks and envelopes slid off my worktable.

A poplar separating vineyards whispered over
olive and lavender cotton, two shades of summer brown.

Wind makes my head ache. I long for water
surfaces, light on four different riverbanks,

silver trembling on the edge, a waterfall
come up inside me as I come down to you.

Early to the train station; slow bus back through Monday-
        shuttered towns;
nectarines under the poplar, wind in the quince tree.

For K. J., Leaving and Coming Back

August first: it was a year ago
we drove down from St.-Guilhem-le-Désert
to open up the house in St. Guiraud

rented unseen. I'd stay; you'd go; that's where
our paths diverged. I'd settle down to work,
you'd start the next month of your *Wanderjahr*.

I turned the iron key in the rusted lock
(it came, like a detective-story clue,
in a manila envelope, postmarked

elsewhere, unmarked otherwise) while you
stood behind me in the midday heat.
Somnolent shutters marked our progress. Two

horses grazed on a roof across the street.
You didn't believe me till you turned around.
They were both old, one mottled gray, one white.

Past the kitchen's russet dark, we found
bookshelves on both sides of the fireplace:
Verlaine, *L'Étranger, Notes from the Underground.*

Through an archway, a fresh-plastered staircase
led steeply upward. In a white room stood
a white-clad brass bed. Sunlight in your face

came from the tree-filled window. "You did good."
We laid crisp sheets we would inaugurate
that night, rescued from the *grenier* a wood-

en table we put under the window. Date
our homes from that one, to which you returned
the last week of August, on a late

bus, in shorts, like a crew-cut, sunburned
bidasse. Sunburned, in shorts, a new haircut,
with Auden and a racing pulse I'd earned

by "not being sentimental about
you," I sprinted to "La Populaire."
You walked into my arms when you got out.

At a two-minute bus stop, who would care?
"La Populaire" puffed onward to Millau
while we hiked up to the hiatus where

we'd left ourselves when you left St. Guiraud
after an unambiguous decade
of friendship, and some months of something new.

A long week before either of us said
a compromising word acknowledging
what happened every night in the brass bed

and every bird-heralded blue morning
was something we could claim and keep and use;
was, like the house, a place where we could bring

our road-worn, weary selves.
                                          Now, we've a pause
in a year we wouldn't have wagered on.
Dusk climbs the tiled roof opposite; the blue's

still sun-soaked; it's a week now since you've gone
to be a daughter in the capital.
(I came north with you as far as Beaune.)

I cook things you don't like. Sometimes I fall
asleep, book open, one A.M., sometimes
I long for you all night in Provençal

or langue d'oc, or wish I could, when I'm
too much awake. My early walk, my late
walk mark the day's measures like rhyme.

(There's nothing that I hate—perhaps I hate
the adipose deposits on my thighs
—as much as having to stay put and wait!)

Although a day alone cuts tight or lies
too limp sometimes, I know what I didn't know
a year ago, that makes it the right size:
owned certainty; perpetual surprise.

Celles

for Julie Fay

We liked its name: those ones, feminine plural.
We imagined the abandoned village
inhabited by sisters and sororal

friends, restoring walls and foliage.
Each house could have a window on the lake
that now were ruins on the shore: a pillaged

battleground, the site of an earthquake
softened by bushes like a cemetery?
Evacuated by decree, to make

a giant oxbow where there was a valley.
The water licked the town limits and stopped.
The town was saved from drowning, but kept empty.

One evening's rhythms let us interrupt
a drive toward dinner in Lodève, to swerve
down where a gouged raw path made an abrupt

plunge toward water, following the curve
of red clay foothills, Mississippian,
to test your four-wheel drive, or test your nerve,

you said, when we were safely parked. The sun
glare, behind the windshield, gilt the swells
of water. We got out. Your Indian

print dress blew back around you: your hair fell
glowing across your throat. "You ought to be
painted like that, the patron saint of *Celles*

qui vagabondent autour d'une autre vie."
Scrub oak reclaimed what once was the café.
Swallows swooped through what once was the *mairie,*

banked into a thermal, veered halfway
across the water, toward a thicketed
dusk-dappled hill, then back, elegant play

of gliders celebrant above our heads,
spiraling in the current's arabesque.
"If we were the evacuees," you said,

"it wouldn't be so fucking picturesque
to live in Clermont in an HLM.
They were the last ones anybody asked

"if making up this place was good for them.
And we are making them up, just as much
as sorceresses flocked here for its name."

We made our way through nascent underbrush
to climb the mayor's ragweed-shattered stairs.
Elbow to elbow, though we didn't touch,

we stood on the wind-littered terrace, where
we watched the sun continue its descent.
We drove away before it disappeared

leaving Those Ones lapped by revenant
shadows, now the cicadas' choral
song broke for nightfall, leaving Celles silent
like us, feminine, plural, transient.

Separate Lives

The last time I talked to you in my head
was July third, 1986,
in Paris. It was four A.M. A slick
Brazilian singer at Bercy instead
of dinner, last train home. The unmade bed
reproached me, and the lamp I had to fix
whose feeble current threw a ghostly flick-
er up and down the pages as I read,
a contrapuntal subordinate clause
to every sentence. Starting to dog-ear
my page in *Souvenirs Pieux*, I told
you what and why I thought of Yourcenar,
then blubbered out loud like a six-year-old
"Come home!" although I didn't know where that was.

If you'd gone home, I didn't know where that was
—not uptown, Languedoc, or the Marais
for you, wherever you were. All that day
I'd checked off errands that a person does
at home. Six months before, I'd wept across
just about every street in the *troisième*.
I felt like a surveyor marking them
with snot and tears. Home is where work and loss
intersect until they feel like life.
I lived on that street for as many seasons
as I had lived with you. Nobody's wife
clocked the barges in through harbor grass.
A hard-on has no conscience. Neither has
heartbreak. I didn't want to know your reasons.

Hard break I didn't want: to know your reasons
couldn't have made it easier, or could
it? A good cry beats a rotten mood.
Too good; too bad: she scared herself. Now she's on
her own, third person singular. No frissons
transforming verbs whose "thou" is understood.
Half through the night, almost out of the "would
she hear me testifying on my knees on
this not entirely metaphoric floor"
phase, I wasn't wondering who you were
when, why, where, whether we—no, you—were gone
into the winter when the deejays spun
"You have no right/to ask me how I feel."
As if I'd died and lived to tell the tale.

And if I'd died and lived to tell the tale,
recovered from the knowledge I'd recover,
I looked a little less like death warmed over.
Mist fingering the windowpane of pale
dawn wasn't a ghost child tapping "Fail,"
or, if she was, I wasn't frightened of her.
Morning would find me indisposed to suffer
through haunted coffee reading shadow mail:
the letter forwarded two months too late,
the sonnet sequence in a magazine
which wasn't, though it might have been, about
the face on facing page not facing mine,
the Wite-Out in the next-to-the-last line,
the message on your answering machine.

The message on your answering machine
was "Wing it"—something like "Go, fly, be free."
I chinked my dime through the cacophony
of Twenty-Third and Sixth. It played again.
That was the week of leftovers and mean
songs. You'd asked to borrow back your key.
You probably were where you said you'd be.
You probably wouldn't have let me in.
Then Friday night was Sunday afternoon,
the time I didn't know was the last time
you took me in your mouth and made me come,
you took your looseleaf, and a cab downtown.
Now a phone call costs more than a dime.
There were some changes in the interim.

There were some changes in the interim
since you left, since I ran out of tears,
since I ran into you after three years.
The corners of your eyes, behind pale-rimmed
glasses are wet, flood, meltdown. My hands trem-
ble now, yours too. It's cold as hell in here.
The private parts I have behind my ears
fill up when words slow down and handle them,
but I'm too close to home to need a ride.
I don't know if you have the words I need.
I know you didn't need the ones I had.
Would it have come out better than it did
if I had played it on the other side,
if I had shut the book and understood?

If I had shut the book and understood
I'd reached the end of *Souvenirs Pieux*
whose subtext was a dialogue with you
in absentia, and "gone for good"
just the return address when you replied,
I might have grieved for grief. I only knew
I'd finished crying, and there was a blue-
gray hint of day above the slate outside,
a lunch date about seven hours away.
You've brought me back a book, past grief, half known,
still strange, with your name on it, not the one
I wrote, for me to open where you say
things for yourself, that aren't what you said
the last time I talked to you in my head.

Days of 1944: Three Friends

for Odile Hellier and Geneviève Pastre

I

"It wasn't safe to stay in Saint-Brieuc,
Mother took us across the gash in France,
the rift between langue d'oïl and langue d'oc,
between the Occupation and Pétain's

"lackeys. Her uncle lived near Montpellier.
For a while, my father had good luck.
When he appeared on my second birthday,
we all ate cherries as if they were cake.

"Nine months later, my brother was born.
Then she had three babies on her hands.
My father's letters came, were passed round, torn
and burned. Spies found the Breton Résistance

"or bought someone, nobody can be sure.
My father and my grandmother were shot.
The Germans burned our house. The furniture
was parceled out at auction, lot by lot."

II

"We had to walk from Rodez to Millau.
My sister, with her patent-leather shoes
tied to a string, sat, cried, and wouldn't go
farther. I was ten. I walked, I knew,

"I thought, what it was like to want to die
when we stopped. People waited in the Gare
where no more trains went. I found one bench I
stretched out on. 'I don't care,' I said, 'we are

" 'hungry already.' When my cousin came,
my mother had to hit me to dislodge
me. Only one more mile. The rain
gave the stiff winter houses camouflage

"uniforms. I followed the cousin, numb
as a stone. My sister's shoes shone, two
crystals. I'd left my fossil box at home.
But that was nothing. Just what we lived through."

III

"I was a walking baby in the Bronx.
My astigmatic father was 4-F.
Mother saved bacon grease in coffee cans
for ration points. She was an orphan—*trefe*

"and kosher didn't matter. We were Jews
I knew, before I tried to learn to read—
and that we lived on Eastburn Avenue,
and that you grew a baby from a seed.

"My father's mother's older sister's son
was a pilot, shot down over some
place across the ocean with an un-
familiar vowel. Near where she came from.

"I saw his picture. In his peaked hat he
looked like the soldiers on the magazine
covers. I only knew a Nazi
was bad. I didn't know, if I had been

"born who I was, *there* . . . They said no one knew.
I know the countries, not the counties or
towns my grandparents left—whose other Jews
the fire took, while you lived, I played, at war."

For Jean Migrenne

Mauve into purple, bent on foam-green stems,
a bank of lavender washed by the rain
recalls Languedoc, though this is on the plain
of Caen, between two blocks of HLMs.
Down south, the hedge around the one *lycée*
is rosemary, high as a young girl's eyes.
Here, notebooks bloat in puddles on the grass:
school's out, and has been out for seven days.
Cahiers au feu, le maître au milieu!
My friend's an English teacher, but he knows
more about setting words on fire than those
book-burning kids gone summer-savage do.
Man, woman, *gouine* and *pédé*, Jew, white and Black:
our language is annealed, transmuted, changed
out of our many, into his mother tongue
that will be ours because he brought us back,
faithful, into the words he earned with need.
His uncles followed herds and farmed the rocks
for earth apples, drank hard. There were no books.
The scrubbed boy went to school and learned to read.
He learned to read the rocks that, aeons old,
have lives inscribed in layers beneath the schist.
He learned how to become an alchemist
who turns the New World's ore to Gallic gold.
Metaphor the solvent, words dissolve
and crystallize again in the alembic.
Alexandrine clusters replace iambic
pentameters; crystals of ten-turned-twelve
glow, faceted, in readers' eyes, where I've
seen my own sea-changed lines catch light. As if
the words acknowledged him for their new life

they lead him back into their other lives:
Josephine Baker's Black gold in the sleaze
light of a nightclub for expatriates,
heroin dawns in Lower East Side squats,
revival-tent hot nights in Mississippi's
swamp country, cities of the dead in Queens,
kosher food, soul food, the Black Bourgeoisie
whose son, running, with blameless grocery
bags, home, is shot by cops. He was sixteen.
The translator haunts him in rituals
performed by cliques in lunchrooms and study halls,
the semiology of toilet stalls.
The translator transforms someone's first menses,
first neutral pronouns and conditional tenses,
first systematic derangement of the senses.
He feels his way along a knot of words
tangled with anger, music, grief, love, play.
Some local teenaged daredevil has spray-
painted *Je T'Aime* on a peeling billboard's
Fiat—no proper name, so no dispute—
where we retrace our path, carrying bread
for lunch, and argue meters as we head
across the road that feeds the autoroute.

Going Back to the River

for K. J.

Dusk, iridescent gasoline floats on the
rain puddles, peacock feathers on macadam.
Schoolgirl beneath an awning pulls her
collar up, here comes her bus. She's gone now.

Nine-thirty, and there's light behind thunderheads.
Storm over, in an hour it will rain again.
Meal done, across the street a neighbor
shakes out her tablecloth from the window.

I have a reading lamp and an open book.
Last glass of wine, last morsel of Saint-André
prolong my dinner and my chapter
into the ten o'clock Haydn program.

What will I say to you when I write to you?
(What would I say to someone who isn't you?)
I'm home, I've cleaned the kitchen, taken
charge of my solitude, taken long baths.

What do I tell myself when I open and
write in the notebook keeping me company?
Don't stay indoors tomorrow morning.
Do the week's shopping at Sunday market.

Go to the river, take what it offers you.
When you were young, it guarded and promised you
that you would follow other rivers
oceans away from a landlocked childhood.

Yes, I indulge myself in hyperbole
since I'm not going out for a walk in this
    wet weather, though I'd walk from someone
    else's place, stop on the bridge, look over.

Seine, Thames and Hudson (sounds like a publisher):
one river flows down into another one.
    Where did I sit and read alone, who
    walked with me which afternoon, which evening?

There was a river when I was leaving you.
That morning, with our *café con leche,* we
    slouched on a bench above the Hudson,
    washed in the wind of a near departure.

Not rupture: each one went where she had to go.
Still, I'd be hours and borders away from you.
    We bluffed like adolescent soldiers
    at the significant bridge or crossroad.

"Your father," you said, "would have been proud of you."
"My mother never would have imagined it."
    Poor Jews in an antagonistic
    city, they pulled in their walls around them.

One city would have looked like another one:
hard work, a clean house, food without seasoning.
    Scrub Europe from a neutral palate,
    blend and assimilate, mistrust strangers,

know in an instant which are the *lanzmänner.*
No Yiddish pet names, gossip or baby talk.
    Brownshirts outside the door would pass on
    innocent, bland Mid-Atlantic Standard.

Is any accent that safely nondescript?
Their child, I bruise my brain on two languages
　　(neither the one they lost) four decades
　　after they earned me this freedom, passing

as what they weren't: rooted American.
Their daughter, I come home to two continents,
　　live with my roots tied up in parcels,
　　still impecunious, maybe foolish.

Another child of children of immigrants
(Russian, Italian), you've chosen languages
　　written in symbols meant to have no
　　country of origin, color, gender

(though every symbol's chiseled with history).
There, you are learning chemical formulae:
　　meals on the run, a book you started
　　months ago under the bed, abandoned.

Life's not forever, love is precarious.
Wherever I live, let me come home to you
　　as you are, I as I am, where you
　　meet me and walk with me to the river.

Against Silence

for Margaret Delany

Because you are
my only daughter's only grandmother,
because your only grandchild is my child
I would have wished you to be reconciled

to how and what
I live. No name frames our connection, not
"in-laws." I hoped, more than "your son's ex-wife."
I've known you now for two-thirds of my life.

You had good friends,
good books, good food, good manners, a good mind.
I was fifteen. I wished this were my home.
(None of my Jewish aunts read *I. F. Stone's*

Weekly, or shopped at Saks
Fifth Avenue, none of them grew up Black
working poor, unduped and civilized.)
I know you were unpleasantly surprised

when, eighteen, we
presented you with the fait accompli
of courthouse marriage in one of two states
where no age-of-consent or miscegenat-

ion laws applied.
Your sister's Beetle—bumps knife thrusts inside
after a midnight Bellevue D and C—
brought me uptown. You took care of me,

a vomit-green
white girl in your son's room. Had I been
pregnant? Aborted? No. Miscarried? Yes.
You didn't ask. I didn't tell, just guessed

what you knew. You
asked my mother to lunch. I'd "had the flu."
She greeted me, "Your hair looks like dog shit.
Cut it or do something to it!"

I burned with shame
you saw what kind of family I came
from. Could you imagine me more
than an unacceptable daughter-in-law?

When, fortified,
I went home to the Lower East Side,
my new job, art school at night and my queer
marriage, you were, understandably, there.

For a decade's
holidays, there was always a place
set for me, if I was in New York.
Your gifts groomed me: a dark-green wool for work

pinstriped Villager
shirts. I brought books, wine, an Irish mohair
shawl laced with velvet ribbons. I came back
from London with a kangaroo-pouch pack

containing your
exuberant golden granddaughter.
You never asked me why I lived alone
after that. Feast-day invitations

stopped—Iva went
with her father. Evenings you spent
with friends, but normal Sundays you'd be in.
I'd call, we'd come a little before noon.

Because you did
that, Sundays there'd be fried liver or shad
roe, or bacon, hot rolls, hash, poached eggs.
We ate while Iva tugged around our legs

the big plush bear
you gave her. From the pile beside your chair
I picked over, passed you the book reviews
in exchange for White Sales and the "News

of the Week in
Review." Your mother, ninety-eight, deep in
somnolent cushions, eighty years' baker of rolls,
wakened by child noise, called the child, and told

her stories
nine decades vivid, linking the rose-gold three-
year-old, British born, Black by law
and choice as she was, with diaspora

Virginia, Harlem;
linking me, listening beside them
with you. She died at one hundred and two
and I, childlike, took it for granted you

would certainly
be bad-mouthing Republicans with me
for two more decades' editorial page.
Seventy-four was merely middle age.

The question some
structuralist with me on a podium,
exalted past politeness, called *"idiote"*
(a schoolyard-brawl word) "For whom do you write?"

I could have answered
(although it wouldn't have occurred
to anyone to ask it after that),
"I write for somebody like Margaret"

—but I'd written
names for acts and actors which, by then,
reader, you'd read, and read me out, abhorred
in print lives you'd let live behind closed doors.

You wouldn't be
in that debate, agree to disagree.
We would need time, I thought. This can resume,
like any talk, with fresh air in the room

and a fresh pot
of coffee, in the fall. But it will not.
Some overload blocked silence in your brain.
A starched girl starts your syllables again.

You held your tongue
often enough to hear, when you were young,
and older, more than you wanted to discuss.
Some things were more acceptable, nameless.

You sometimes say
names amidst the glossolalial
paragraphs that you enunciate
now, unanswerable as, "Too late."

Baffled between
intention and expression, when your son
says, "Squeeze my hand, once for 'no,' twice for 'yes,' "
you squeeze ten times, or none, gratuitous.

A hemisphere
away from understanding where you are,
mourning your lost words, I am at a loss
for words to name what my loss of you is,
what it will be, or even what it was.

INDEX